SOPRINTENDENZA ARCHEOLOGICA DI ROMA

THE PALATINE

ELECTA

THE HISTORY OF THE HILL
FROM ITS ORIGINS TO ITS REDISCOVERY

«At that hour when the fiery sun had climbed
To heaven's midpoint, distant still they saw
Wall, citadel, a few house tops - the town
Built heavenward by Roman power now
But meager, and poor, held by Evander»
(Virgil, *Aeneid*, VIII, 97-100)

Virgil's account of Aeneas, fleeing from Troy and welcomed by the old king Evander exiled from Arcadia together with his relatives and living on the Palatine Hill, has long been considered a learned reconstruction. Actually, it not only reflects the idea Romans had about their own origins, but surprisingly enough tells us of a reality that to a certain extent excavations have reconfirmed.

Today we know that the Palatine was inhabited from the Middle Palaeolithic era (some 100,000 to 35,000 years ago). More to the point, we now know that already by the 9th century BC (which means a century before Romulus founded Rome, according to tradition) the first settlers had installed themselves on a permanent basis on the hill.

From the beginning of the 1900 onwards, archaeological finds also seem to reconfirm the legend: the hill certainly contained a pre-Romulean settlement, according to Virgil and Dionysius of Halicarnassus. There was a settlement of huts on the crown of the hill

from at least the 8th century BC, a date that coincides with that of the founding of Rome suggested by the ancient authors.

The Palatine Hill, pleasant both for its detached position and its wide open vistas, lies to the east of the Tiber valley. It has a central summit (the *Palatium*) with a top approximately 50 m above sea level, which has been located around the Temple of the *Magna Mater* (Great Mother). The southern slopes of the hill, towards the *Velabrum* and the Circus Maximus, took the name of *Cermalus,* which meant German, and came from the legend of the basket with the twins Romulus and Remus, who were in fact called 'the germans' (Plutarch, *Life of Romulus*, 3, 6).

First a saddle then a ridge called the Velia, separated the Palatine from the Esquiline.

Protected by steep tufaceous rocks, its position close to the Tiber, and near the Tiber Island which allowed for easy access, was perfectly suited for human settlement. Its etymology is uncertain, and very controversial; most of the ancient authors (Dionysius of Halicarnassus, Livy, Pliny, Solinus and others) derive the name *Palatium* from *Pallantion*, the town in Arcadia from which Evander would have come to Italy. Another etymology has also been suggested from the same legend: from Pallantes according to some, Evander's ancestor or son, and

1. A.L.R. Ducros
(18th century),
The Farnese Gardens.
Lausanne, Musée
Cantonal des Beaux-Arts

2. Model of the
Romulean hut discovered
on the Cermalus.
Reconstruction by
A. Davico (1950).
Rome, Museo Palatino

according to others, son of Hercules and Lavinia, who was Evander's daughter.

Varro, Festus and others take the word *Palatium* back to the Goddess *Pales*, patroness of shepherds, who was celebrated annually during the *Palilia* on April 21, Rome's birthday.

According to tradition, the early town was surrounded by walls. Their perimeter, however, is uncertain, and has often been mistaken for that of Square Rome.

Pliny ascribes three gateways to the Palatine (*Natural History*, 3, 5, 66); their locations, actually lost, are hotly disputed amongst archaeologists: the Mugonia Gate, so called from the bellowing of the oxen that passed beneath it, also called *vetus porta Palatii,* "permitted access to the Palatine from the *via Sacra*" (Dionysius of Halicarnassus, 2, 50, 3); the Romana Gate or *Romanula*, as it was called by the Sabines, for it was through this that they entered Rome. Varro locates it close to the *via Nova*, by the *sacellum Volupiae*, while Festus places it on the lower part of the Victory *Clivus*. Both authors mention the presence of *gradus* close by. These indications suggest that the Romana Gate may have been in the north-west corner of the hill, where the steps from the spring of Juturna climbed up to the *via Nova*. The location of the third gateway relates to the *Scalae Caci*, mentioned by Solinus as one of the boundaries of Square Rome.

In the period between the 4th century and the 1st century BC the history of the Palatine remains somewhat obscure. The only pieces of information available to us regard the building of temples. Obviously the sites of the Romulus legend gave the hill religious connotations from earliest times.

It is probable that already in archaic times there were sacred buildings on the summit of the hill, as many of the architectural terracottas and antefixes recovered in this area since the 19th century seem to suggest.

The Temple of Victory has recently been identified by means of excavations. It was dedicated by *Lucius Postumius Megellus* in 294 BC, perhaps over a previously existing shrine to the goddess. Dionysius attributed its founding to Evander. During excavations a great wealth of terracotta finds were unearthed, including fronton statues, facing slabs and polychrome antefixes.

In 191 BC, on the summit of the Palatine Hill, to the west of the Victory *Clivus*, the Temple of the *Magna Mater* Cybele was dedicated, after the Sibylline Books, consulted during the Second Punic War, had prescribed that the non-iconic simulacre of the Goddess, made of a black stone, should be brought to Rome from Pessinus.

Due to the historical and religious importance that the hill had acquired, the Palatine, during the Republican age, became the privileged site for the residences of the Roman upper class.

To have a house on the hill was the great ambition of every important citizen and therefore land values were very high. In the last two centuries of the Republic there were many residences belonging to famous people whose names have come down to us.

Among the most ancient of these was that of *Vitruvius Vaccus*, sentenced in 330 BC for having supported the rebellions of Fondi and Priverno. After the sentence his property was declared public domain and even in Cicero's time there was a public space on the Palatine that went by the name of *Vacci prata*.

Sources also mention the *domus* of *Marcus Fulvius Flaccus*, consul in 125 BC; that of *Quintus Lutatius Catulus*, consul in 102 BC; that of *Lucius Crassus* the orator, and that of *Marcus Livius Drusus*, tribune of the people in 91 BC.

Marcus Tullius Cicero gives us

3. *Head of a divinity, possibly Zeus (beginning of the 3rd century BC). From the site of the Temple of Victory. Rome, Museo Palatino*

information about the house he owned and also about the one owned by his brother *Quintus* on the hill. Two fierce political rivals, *Titus Annius Milo* and *Publius Clodius*, also owned important properties on the Palatine as well as *Marcus Aemilius Scaurus*, Sulla's step-son. Also worth mentioning at the end of the Republican age are the properties of *Marcus Antonius*, the famous triumvir; that of *Publius Cornelius Silla*, nephew to the dictator; *Gaius Licinius Calvus*, another important orator; *Marcus Vipsanius Agrippa*, Augustus' son in law, whose house, formerly belonged to *Marcus Antonius*, and which after his death became the property of *Marcus Valerius Messala Corvinus*. Finally there were the residences of *Germanicus*, emperor Tiberius' nephew, of *Proculus* and of *Quintus Hortensius*. The Palatine was almost completely covered by these luxury *domus* when Augustus decided to establish his own residence there. The *Octavii*, Octavian's paternal family, already owned a small property on the slopes of the hill, near the Velia gate, in a place called *ad capita bubula*, where Augustus was born. Octavian himself, had formerly lived above the Annular Steps – the site has not clearly been identified, but was certainly close to the Forum – in a house that once belonged to the orator *Calvus*. In 23 BC Augustus, having only recently been appointed to the *tribunicia potestas* for life, decided to set up his residence on the Palatine, purchasing the house of the orator Hortensius, which was to become the first nucleus of his property. The choice of the site, on the summit of the *Cermalus*, close by the house of Romulus and the other sacred sites related to Rome's foundation, was, apart from the importance of the place itself, motivated by the tie Octavian felt to his place of birth; and above all by his desire to revive within his fellow Romans the cult of their origins.

Following Augustus' example, his successor Tiberius also chose the Palatine as his place of residence. His name is bound with that of the *Domus Tiberiana*, a building that exists to this

day above the Forum, in the north-west corner of the hill, completely covered by the Farnese Gardens. He was in turn followed by Caligula, who extended Tiberius' palace right up to the Forum, to the Temple of the Castors (*Domus Gai*).

It is uncertain whether the emperor Claudius was engaged in major building activities on the hill; but under his successor Nero, architectural dimensions, building criteria and even the town-planning of the whole area underwent major transformations.

Nero's work on the Palatine started with the construction of the *Domus Transitoria*. These remarkable remains are to be found under the Triclinium of the *Domus Flavia*. After its destruction, in the fire of 64 AD, the emperor conceived and partially built a vast new residence, the *Domus Aurea* that began on the Palatine and stretched as far as the Esquiline, and

4. Archaic antefix of a female head from the site of the House of the Griffins. Rome, Museo Palatino

5. Polychrome terracotta plate depicting a chariot race (6th century BC). From the site of the Temple of Victory. Rome, Museo Palatino

about which the ancient sources left us admirable descriptions.

But the most radical transformation of the hill came from the Flavians. Domitian's vast project, carried out by his architect Rabirius, filled in the valley between the *Palatium* and the *Cermalus*, and on top of the existing buildings built a grand and sumptuous residence. Martial refers to this as *Parrhasia*, and, from the site on which it rose, took the name of *Palatium*, that is to say the Palace out of excellency, a term still used in many languages to this day (*Palais, Palazzo)* to indicate any prestigious building.

To provide the Palatine with the necessary water, Domitian extended the aqueduct of *Aqua Claudia* from the Caelian hill. Afterwards he intervened on the eastern spur of the hill facing the valley of the Coliseum. There he built a great terrace, perhaps designed as a garden (the Barberini Vineyard). Furthermore the emperor, after the fire of AD 80, rebuilt the northern front of the *Domus Tiberiana* and, on a massive scale, the buildings close to the Temple of the Castors, which served as an entrance hall to the Imperial Palaces when approaching from the Forum.

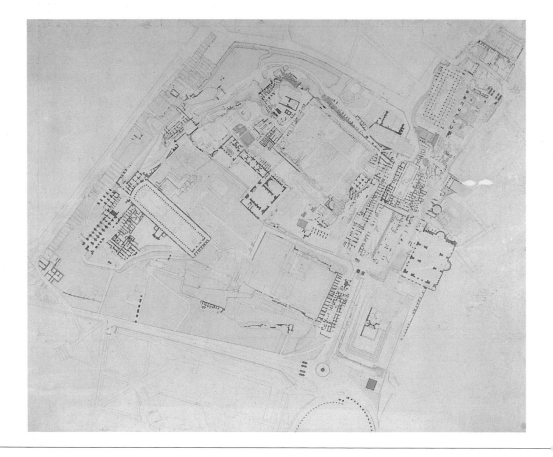

6. Plan of the Forum and the Palatine by M. Giammiti (1895). Rome, Museo Palatino

7. M. Granet (1802-1824). Le Palais des Empereurs. Aix en Provence, Musée Granet

The emperors Trajan and Hadrian do not appear to have ever lived permanently on the Palatine. However, under Hadrian, building work on the hill must have been intense as virtually every monument bears his mark. After Hadrian, building work ceased for nearly a century.

Work started energetically again under Septimius Severus. In fact the great Baths seem to date back to him. With a series of arcades of two orders, he extended the level of the hill towards the south, until it practically reached the steps of the Circus Maximus. Upon these artificial platform he built a colossal thermal plant that extended so far out that it nearly touched the exhedra of the Stadium. A large theatrical box overlooked the Circus Maximus, from which the imperial family could comfortably enjoy the performances, with the 250,000 spectators of the Circus at their feet.

Near the Baths he built the magnificent monumental facade of the *Septizodium* to impress all those entering Rome from the Appian Way.

Parts of the Palace logistical support spaces, those situated on the southern slopes bordering on the Circus Maximus, can also be dated to the time of Septimius Severus, or perhaps a little later. They are the so-called *Schola Praecon-um*, with its important paintings; and the *Pedagogium* with its well known graffiti.

After Septimius Severus, no other building work of any importance was carried out on the Palatine, being by then completely built up.

The only exception was the Temple of Elagabalus built on the eastern terrace facing the Coliseum. This building was dedicated to the Sun, and within it were gathered all the most sacred objects of Rome.

When finally the imperial headquarters were transferred to Constantinople, under Constantine, the Palatine came into decline, though it housed the imperial residence and remained the official seat of representation for the Eastern Emperors.

The Regionary Catalogues, compiled in the time of Constantine, listed on the *Palatium* – which constituted the X of the Augustan regions – 20 *vici* or quarters; 20 *aedicules compitales*; 2742 *insulae*; 89 grand houses; 48 *horrea;* 49 public baths; 90 fountains and 20 mills. The perimeter of the region was nearly four kilometres in length.

The monuments of the Palatine mentioned in the Catalogues as existent in the 4th century are: the Hut of Romulus; the Temple of Apollo

and the Temple of the *Magna Mater*; the *Pentapylum*; the *Domus Augustana* and the *Tiberiana*; the *Auguratorium*; the Temple of Jupiter; the *Curiae Veteres*; the *Fortuna Respiciens*; the *Septizodium*; the *Victoria Germaniciana*; the Lupercal; the Palatine area and the *Domus Dionis* (of the latter nothing is known).

An inscription *in foro Palatini* of the emperors Valens, Valentinian and Gratian, transcribed at the end of the 8th century AD by a pilgrim from Einsiedeln, offers documentary evidence that these emperors donated part of the hill to the people of Rome, under the care of a town prefect. In the Middle Ages, information about the Palatine is very scarce. It is known that the barbarian kings Odoacer and Theodoric lived there to give their power greater formality, and that in 629 AD the Senate, assembled in the *Domus Flavia*, solemnly received the Emperor Heraclius.

At a later date, when imperial power was substituted by papal power, some of the Popes also chose to live there, even though only occasionally.

During Byzantine domination, the Palatine was the seat of the Roman *dux*. It was during this period that the first signs of a monastic presence on the hill were made known.

The oldest evidence of Christianity on the Palatine is the Church of San Cesario that, in its capacity of Palatine Chapel, substituted what once had been the *Lararium* of the Imperial Palace. In the 9th century a Greek monastery was built nearby, the importance of which must have grown in the course of centuries, for Eugene III was elected Pope there in 1145.

At the foot of the *Domus Tiberiana*, inside the large Domitian halls that opened onto the Forum, the Church of Santa Maria Antiqua was also built. It was richly decorated with a very important pictorial cycle.

The Monastery of Santa Maria in Pallara also stood on the terrace in the direction of the Coliseum valley. It was named so, it seems, in memory of the Palladium that Elagabalus had left in the nearby Temple of the Sun. It was to this church (which from the middle of the 14th century onwards was perhaps the seat of the abbot of Montecassino) that the cult of Saint Sebastian was associated, from an early date, because according to late sources, he was martyred there, or to be more precise nearby on the Temple steps (*gradus Helagabali*). However, it was not in the interior of the hill, now depopulated and in decay, that Christianity secured a foothold but in marginal areas, closer to where people were still living.

The *Septizodium* was added to the nearby Abbey of San Gregorio, that subsequently occupied even the Severan Baths, called Minor *Septizodium*. Still in the south-eastern corner of the hill, there stood the little Church, that today no longer exists, of Santa Lucia in Septisolio. A fresco with the figures of saints, from the 9th century, was recently discovered in a room on the site of the Severan Arcades, and might have been part of the decoration of this little church. On the slopes of the *Velabrum* rose the Church

---

8. Fresco from the pictorial cycle in Santa Maria Antiqua

A visit to the Palatine

«*Rome 10-11 Nov. 1786.* Today I visited the Pyramid of Cestius and in the evening the Palatine, among the ruins of Imperial Palaces that rise up like rock faces. It is impossible to convey all this. True to

say that nothing was done on a small scale (...). These people worked for eternity, and took everything into account, apart from the madness of those who destroy to whom all must yield.»
(J.W. Goethe, *An Italian Journey,* 1786-1788).

9. "The Great Fountain" and one of the Aviaries in the Farnese Gardens

of Sant'Anastasia, mounted on strong building blocks. The diaconate of San Teodoro, yet another Greek saint, stood near the *Horrea Agrippiana*, in the north-western corner of the hill. During the 11th and the 12th centuries a large part of the hill became a fortress belonging to the Frangipane family: a long turreted wall, the conspicuous ruins of which can be seen mostly around the *Velabrum*, surrounded the Palatine from the Arch of Titus to the Church of San Teodoro, including several ancient constructions. The stronghold of the Frangipane's fortification was the *Turris Chartularia*, where for a long time the Church's archives were kept. The tower, not far from the Arch of Titus, was demolished by Valadier in 1829: it is important to remember that in 1167 Pope Alexander III took refuge there from the supporters of Federico Barbarossa. In 1118 Gelasio II, a pope of the Caetani family, was elected to the papal throne in the nearby Monastery of Santa Maria in Pallara.

In the first centuries after the year One Thousand, the Palatine was often the theatre for ferocious fighting among the powerful Roman families, until a sort of oblivion fell over it, which lasted until the Renaissance.

The Renaissance saw the hill covered with vineyards and gardens, belonging to the Roman aristocracy. The site of the Stadium was occupied by the Roncioni family; the Severan buildings by the English College, while the western slope towards the Circus Maximus was shared between the Nusiner and the Butirroni families. The Barberini became owners of the eastern terrace, that looked out over the valley of the Amphitheatre. In the centre of the Palatine, above the Flavians Palace, the Stati family installed itself; followed by the Mattei, the Spada, the Magnani, the Rancoureil, and the Scotsman Charles Mills.

The most splendid gardens belonged to the Farnese, and were created by Cardinal Alexander Farnese above the *Domus Flavia* and the *Domus Tiberiana*.

A history of the excavations

Excavations on the Palatine first began in the Renaissance, but only in an unsystematic way. They were carried out in order to improve the princely gardens and recuperate works of art either for private collections or for sale. About these first rummagings, for the most part ruinous, we have scarce and fragmentary information, gleaned from the contracts of excavations or sale of that time. Other and not always reliable information is provided from the notes of famous artists such as Bramante, Palladio, Ligorio, Dosio, Flaminio Vacca, Van Heemskerck, Panvinio, who have handed down important testimonies as to the state of the "Major Palace", as the Flavians Palace was referred to at that time. The plan by Andrea Palladio, as Rodolfo Lanciani recalls, is one of the most interesting, even though he confuses the Imperial Palace with a thermal complex.

Important discoveries of works of art were made in the 16th and 17th centuries.

Plundering raids were often ordered by the popes themselves: in 1552 a ransacking expedition was organised by the Roncioni family, who sold cipolin marble columns, pedestals, bases, and even the marble gutter from the portico roof to Pope Julius III.

Flaminio Vacca speaks of twenty statues of Amazons that were unearthed and removed from the Stadium. Many believed these to be the famous Danaides that once decorated the portico of the Temple of Apollo. Vacca speaks also of a basalt head of Capitoline Jupiter as well as of the famous Hercules by Lysippus, purchased by Cosimo III Medici for exhibition in Florence.

In 1588-1589, pope Sistus V had his architect Domenico Fontana demolish what remained of the *Septizodium*. Most of this had already been destroyed in 1257 by senator Brancaleone. The work cost the pope 905 *scudi*, but was very adaquately compensated for from the acquisition of columns, peperino, travertine and rare marble slabs.

In 1664 – according to Lanciani in his work dedicated to the history of the excavations – in the in-

10. Statue of Hercules in basalt from the 18th century excavations. Parma, Pinacoteca Nazionale

terior of the *Domus Augustana*, at that time the property of the Mattei family, "a portico of extraordinary preciosity was discovered. It had *giallo antico* columns and two bas-reliefs representing Romulus, Remus, the She-wolf, the Lupercal, Faustulus, the Tiber and other subjects related to the founding of Rome."

In 1728, count Spada, who had purchased the property from the Mattei, discovered seven rooms "decorated with precious marbles, golden bronze, stuccoes on a golden background, and rich vegetable embellishments. In another room used as a bathroom, was found a *cathedra* in marble with a led basin in front of it. The two columns of oriental alabaster standing on each side of the *cathedra* were removed and placed in the chapel of Prince Odescalchi in the church of Santi Apostoli." "Broken statues of marble and bronze" were also found. In the 18th century the first systematic excavations were begun by order of Francis I, duke of Parma, who in 1720 had become the owner of the Farnese Gardens. The documentation of the excavations, which lasted on and off up until 1729, was carried

out by the abbot Francesco Bianchini, who was then Commissary for Antiquities. It was published posthumously in 1738. During that time the *Domus Flavia* was excavated as well as other constructions below (the *Aula Isiaca*, the House of the Griffins and the *Domus Transitoria*). These latter excavations were afterwards covered over. Investigations were also carried out on the *Domus Tiberiana*, the House of Livia – where paintings from one of the rooms were removed – and on some limited areas in the Farnese Gardens.

The very refined paintings found in the *Domus Transitoria* have partially ended up in Naples, in the store rooms of the Archaeological Museum; of them we have a good water colour documentation of the time. Others were removed and sent to Parma, as for example the basalt colossi of Hercules and Bacchus, which are still housed in the art gallery of that city.

About half a century later, in 1775, the French abbot Rancoureil undertook a large scale excavation in the lower peristyle of the *Domus Augustana*, which was carried out in great secrecy. Three large

11. Fresco from the Domus Transitoria reproduced in a water-colour by F. Bartoli in 1721.
The Topham Collection, Eton College, Windsor

rooms abutting onto the cut of the hill, with mixtilinear plan, were brought to light together with all the rooms of the *Domus* that looked out onto the Circus Maximus. The dig was without question an act of vandalism, and was carried out exclusively for the sake of gain. The important sculptural material recuperated was either sold or lost (this included two statues of Leda and the swan, and the Sauroktonos Apollo today in the Vatican Museums). Only through the zeal of Rancoureil's young assistant, the architect Barberi, was it possible to obtain a plan of the excavation, however inaccurate, which was later edited by Guattani.

In 1828 the architect to the Court of Russia named Constantine Thon published seven important tables about the Palace of the Caesars on the Palatine, with a brief explanatory text by Vincenzo Ballanti.

In 1835, some areas investigated by Francesco Bianchini were re-excavated by the king of Naples, but with no important result.

In the years 1845-1847 various surveys were carried out by Vescovali in the area between the *Pedagogium* and the Church of San Teodoro. In 1846 other explorations were conducted by the crown of Russia in the Nusiner and Butirroni Vineyards, not far from the Church of Sant'Anastasia. However, the excavations were curtailed soon afterwards as the art objects recuperated were not regarded as being of great importance.

In 1861, having purchased the Farnese Gardens from Francis II Bourbon, the former king of Naples, Napoleon III entrusted the survey to Pietro Rosa, pupil of Luigi Canina. The ensuing excavations, which lasted until 1870, were the most important carried out on the Palatine up until that time. They unearthed the *Clivus Palatinus* and the Temple that Pietro Rosa believed to be of Jupiter Stator. Large parts of the *Domus Tiberiana* were excavated mostly along the northern, eastern and southern fronts, and along Nero's cryptoporticus. Most of the *Domus Flavia* was dug as far as the Domitian Libraries, including the *intermontium* that separated the *Cermalus* from the *Palatium*, an area that had been filled in by the Flavians. Also excavated were the Temple of Apollo, identified by Rosa as that of Jupiter the Victorious, the Temple of the *Magna Mater*, the House of Livia, the *Scalae Caci*, and the archaic cistern.

These very extensive excavations allowed for the recovery of much important material, mostly sculptural, from which the first Antiquarium of the Palatine was put together by Rosa, on the ground floor of an existing Farnese building inside the *Domus Tiberiana*. Rosa's greatest merit was for having introduced more accurate and serious criteria in his procedure, his goal being not just the re-

Plundering excavations at the *Domus Transitoria*

«The stairway walls and those in the room were covered with beautiful frescos, of which not even a square centimetre was saved. Fortunately they had been copied by Gaetano Piccini and Francesco Bartoli (...). They depicted rural motifs, sacrifices, Bacchic dances, all bursting with gracious figures. When one reflects that these artistic masterpieces from the time of Domitian were found unbroken in the first quarter of the last century, in the presence of such people as Cardinal Alessandro Albani, Pier Leone Ghezzi, Francesco Bianchini and Francesco Bartoli; and that these same walls that supported the frescos were demolished in order to sell the bricks, one asks oneself what right do we have to go on blaming the Middle Ages or the Barbarians for acts far less shameful than this» (From R. Lanciani, *Rovine e scavi di Roma antica*, Roma 1897).

covery of the 'beautiful object', but the topographic and historic research related to it.

After the Papal States had acquired a great part of the Palatine properties, the archaeologists Grifi and Visconti, under Pio IX, dug large areas of the Severan complex and of the Palatine Stadium between 1865 and 1868, recovering a rich hoard of artefacts which were carried back to the Vatican.

Under the wise mediation of Rosa, the Farnese Gardens were handed over by Napoleon III, and after 1870 the Palatine became the property of the Italian State through a series of purchases and expropriations, the last being those of the Villa Mills (with its adjoining Convent of the Visitation) in 1906, and the Barberini Vineyard in 1909.

Following the unification of Italy, archaeological explorations received a new impulse. Between 1871 and 1878 the Stadium was excavated together with the exhedra and the access stairway into the Severan Baths. Between 1878 and 1884

Rodolfo Lanciani re-established the topographical continuity between the Forum and the Palatine, by demolishing the boundary wall and the gateway to the Farnese Gardens. In 1886 came the completion of the excavations of the side of the *Domus Tiberiana* facing San Teodoro; followed in 1888 by those of the *Pedagogium* on the via dei Cerchi. In 1892 excavations focused on connecting the Stadium with the *Domus Augustana*.

In 1907 Dante Vaglieri began explorations of the necropolis on the *Cermalus* and of the site of the *Scalae Caci*. Work soon came to a halt, however, following harsh criticism concerning his method of investigation.

Between 1910 and 1914 Giacomo Boni began excavations on the Palatine, in particular those related to the Republican houses under the *Domus Flavia*. He brought to light areas already partially dug by F. Bianchini, such as the House of the Griffins, the *Aula Isiaca* and the remains of Nero's

12. Small statue of Dionysius as a child excavated by P. Rosa on the site of the Farnese Gardens. Rome, Museo Palatino

13. The Palatine Antiquarium, as laid out by P. Rosa (1862)

buildings commonly referred to as the Baths of Livia. The excavations were unfortunately interrupted and the results never published.

Under the direction of Alfonso Bartoli, who succeeded Boni, a very active phase in both excavation and restoration work took place: between 1927 and 1934, after completing the demolition of Villa Mills, already begun by Boni, Bartoli finished the excavation of the *Domus Augustana*. Many important sculptures were recovered. Immediately afterwards, in 1931, he came upon the base of a temple on the terrace of the Barberini Vineyard, perhaps that of Elagabalus. Between 1934 and 1936 he dug the Palatine slopes in the direction of the Velabrum, in search of the Lupercal.

It was also thanks to Bartoli that a new Palatine Antiquarium was established in the former Convent of the Visitation on the summit of the hill.

After an inevitable interruption on account of the Second World War, new excavations began again in the '50s. They were conducted by Pietro Romanelli and Salvatore Puglisi on the *Cermalus* in the same area around the Romulean huts and the Temple of the *Magna Mater*, already partially dug by Vaglieri.

Romanelli, together with the architect Davico, carried out important restoration work in the Farnese Gardens: the Aviaries – converted by Rosa into houses, which he joined together by inserting a central body – were brought back to their original state; the Nymphaeum of the Rain was restored and, after much discussion, the so-called "portal of Vignola", dismantled during the Lanciani excavations, was reassembled and established as an entrance to the Palatine on the side of via di San Gregorio.

The surveys from the mid '60s carried out by Gianfilippo Carettoni on the Augustean site, were very important for the results that they achieved.

14. *Pius IX on a visit to the excavations of the Palatine Stadium in an engraving of that time*

15. *A Farnese building on the Victory Clivus, seat of the first Palatine Antiquarium, set up by P. Rosa in 1862*

Thanks to them, it has been possible to identify the Temple of Apollo with certainty. Furthermore, during the excavations a large section of Augustus' house, with its important pictorial decorations of the Second Style, was brought to light.

Explorations at the *Domus Tiberiana* in the '80s have clarified the chronological phases of the complex. They were begun in the '70s, in the south-western part of the *Cermalus*, around the Temple of the *Magna Mater*, and are still continuing. Also on-going are the explorations of the Palatine slope between the *via Sacra* and the *via Nova*, that are still providing important answers to the archaic phase of primitive Rome. As to other explorations presently underway in the Barberini Vineyard – that were carried out in order to better understand the various stages that this terrace went through from archaic times up until the Middle Ages – these too are nearly concluded.

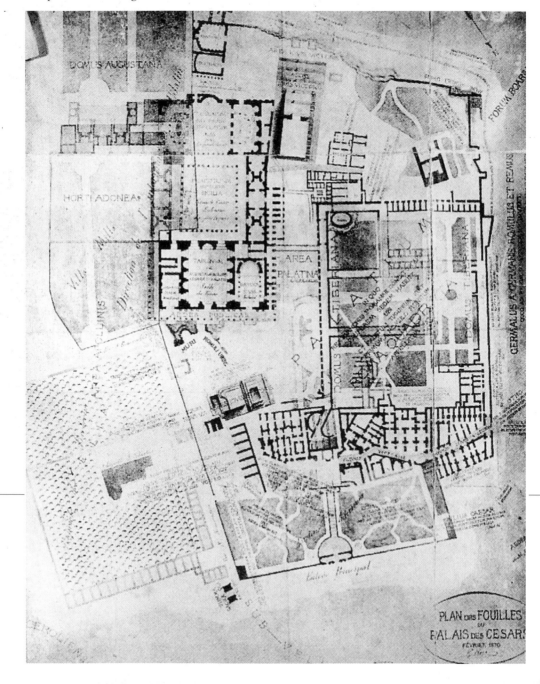

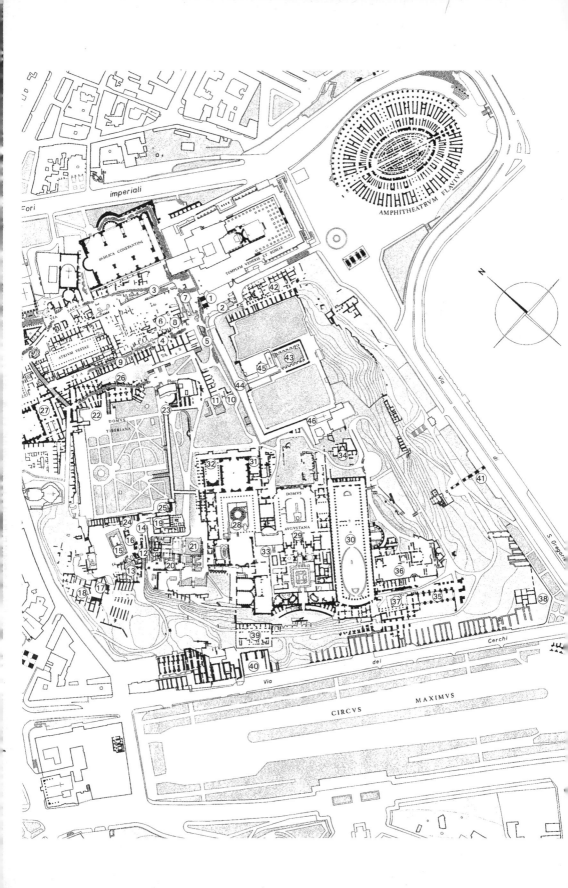

Fori imperiali

BASILICA CONSTANTINI

TEMPLVM VENERIS ET ROMAE

AMPHITHEATRVM FLAVIVM

VIA SACRA

ATRIVM VESTAE

VIA

DOMVS TIBERIANA

DOMVS AVGVSTANA

Via

S. Gregorio

Via di

CIRCVS   MAXIMVS

Cerchi

dei

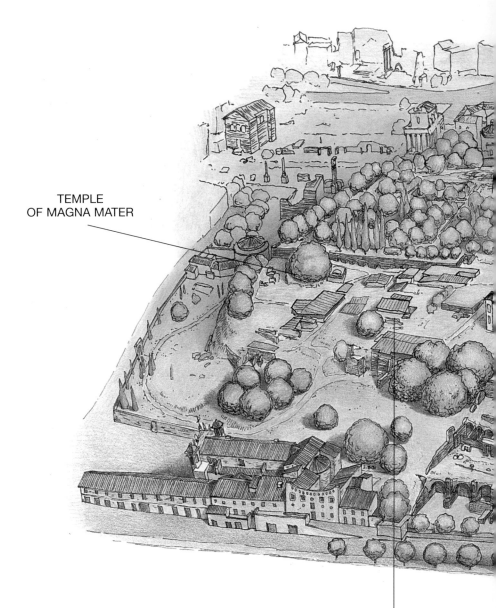

(FARNES
DOMUS

TEMPLE
OF MAGNA MATER

HOUSE OF AUGUSTUS

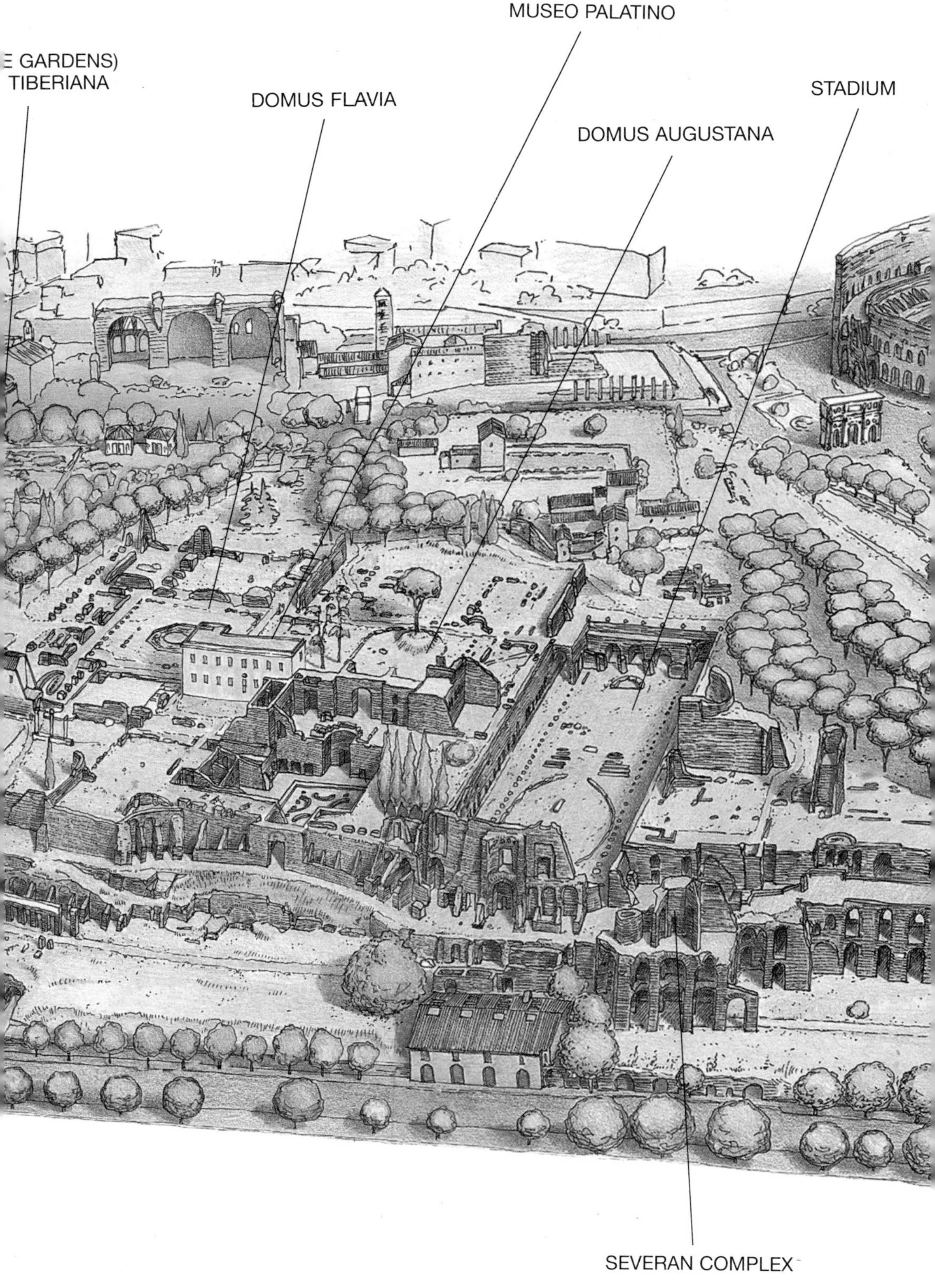

(E GARDENS)
TIBERIANA

DOMUS FLAVIA

MUSEO PALATINO

DOMUS AUGUSTANA

STADIUM

SEVERAN COMPLEX

16. *Excavations in the*
area of the Farnese
Gardens (P. Rosa, Plan
des fouilles du Palais des
Césars, 1870)

17. *Aerial photograph*
of the Palatine after the
excavations of the '30s

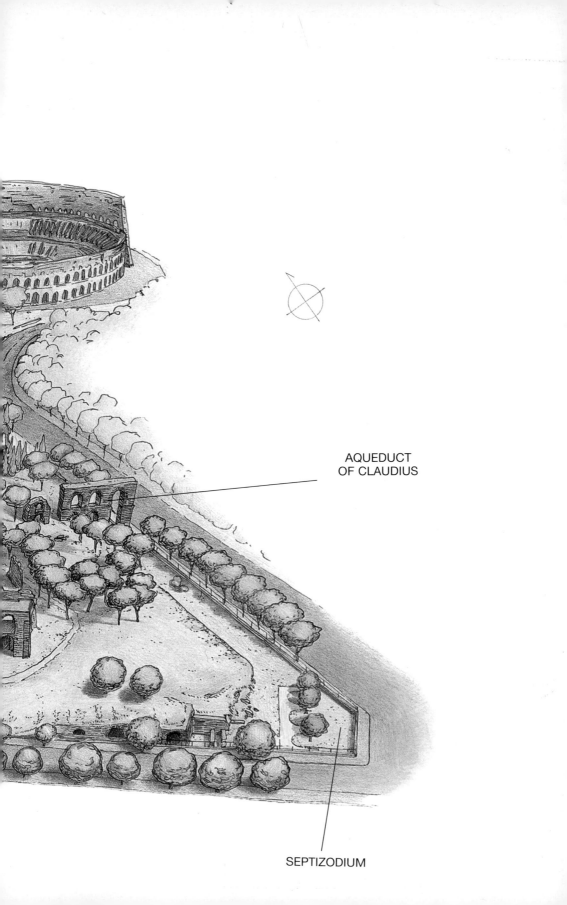

AQUEDUCT
OF CLAUDIUS

SEPTIZODIUM

Suggestions for a visit

It is rather difficult today to understand the monuments on the Palatine Hill, as from Protohistory until the Renaissance, building work has continued upon layer, without any clear distinction between the various periods. To make matters more complicated most of the buildings have lost their external cladding, and brick bases are all that remain of the majority of the temples.
To make the visit easier, this guide intends to follow, wherever possible, an itinerary through chronologically different areas, so as to gain a better understanding of life on the hill through its many historical phases.
The Palatine is reached either from the Roman Forum, or from the other two entrances, one on via di San Gregorio and the other on the side of San Bonaventura. Whatever the case, the visit can always begin at the Arch of Titus.

THE CLIVUS PALATINUS
AND THE NORTHERN SLOPE OF THE HILL

The visit starts at the **Arch of Titus** ①, a single barrel-vault, erected to celebrate the victory of the Romans over the Judaeans and the conquest of Jerusalem by the emperor Titus in AD 70. Two panels in the interior part of the Arch celebrate the most significant episodes of the triumph. To the left, the goddess Roma leads the imperial quadriga, while the emperor is being crowned by a Victory. The right hand side panel depicts the sacred objects of the Jewish religion taken from the Temple in Jerusalem: in the foreground the Jewish seven-branched candelabrum can be seen. The coffered ceiling portrays Titus apotheosis, riding heavenwards on the back of an eagle. In the Middle Ages the Arch was included in the Frangipane's fortification system, and remained as such until the architect Valadier, at the beginning of the 1800s, isolated it with a restoration that provoked more criticism than consensus.
To the east of the Arch can clearly be seen a rectangular foundation **base** ② made of flint chips, with some travertine and peperino blocks leaning against it. The foundation bed – before

recent excavations and studies made excluded this hypothesis – had for a long time been interpreted as being part of the Temple of *Juppiter Stator*, dedicated by Romulus during the Roman-Sabine war. In the Middle Ages, on the remains of this base, the *Turris Chartularia* had been built. It derived its name from the proximity of the *chartularium* (the imperial archives), later to be used by the Popes.
By the Arch of Titus three roads meet: the **via Sacra** ③ coming from the Forum; the **via Nova** ④ of Neronian time, that runs roughly parallel to the *via Sacra,* but further up on the Palatine slope; and the **Clivus Palatinus** ⑤, a name that did not exist in antiquity, but was introduced by Rosa to identify the paved road he had discovered, that branches off from the *via Sacra* opposite the Arch of Titus and climbs up the Palatine. Excavations carried out in the area by Giacomo Boni at the beginning of this century, eliminated the Neronian level of the *via Sacra* and unearthed the more ancient levels below, that date back to Augustan times. As a consequence, the foundations of the Arch of

Titus, built at a later date, are visible to us today.
Further along the *Clivus Palatinus*, the area to the right, between the *via Sacra* and the *via Nova*, is covered by a series of brick walls, parallel to each other and perpendicular to the axis of the *via Sacra*. These walls according to Rodolfo Lanciani are the remains of a large portico that developed around lines of stone pillars. The complex has been identified by Lanicani as the **porticus Margaritaria** ⑥, on the basis of the Cronographer of the year 354, who mentions it as one of the buildings close to the Forum.
Excavations have in fact identified the enormous porticoed structure as having initially been planned by Nero after the fire of 64 AD, which particularly damaged this side of the hill. Following this, Nero wanted to change both the topography and the orientation of this side and began work on a grandiose pillared portico to fill the sides of the *via Sacra* and the *Clivus Palatinus*, intending it to serve as an entrance to the *Domus Aurea*. The ambitious project was never finished. With Nero dead, the Flavians gave the area back to the

18. The Arch of Titus in a reproduction of the 18th century

people and the monumental construction, hardly begun, was remodelled as a *porticus* for public and commercial use, that lasted up until the late Empire. From the Neronian age the only elements remaining are the large **foundations** ⑦ of flint chips that cut through the *via Sacra* and skirt the *Clivus Palatinus*.

The two storey building (one of which is underground) protected by sheds, immediately to the West of the Arch of Titus, is still controversial as to its original function. The thirty or so small rooms in *opus reticulatum*, each 1.80 m by 1.50 m, are symmetrically placed on either side of the corridors and contain only a stone bench on which to sleep and a drain for water. They have been interpreted by some scholars as the *ergastula,* that is to say cells for the slaves of the wealthy **domus** ⑧ above. Other scholars believe them to be an hotel, that also functioned as a brothel (sources mention its existence close to the Forum).

19. Buildings and shops along the via Nova (Neronian period)

20. Entrance to the Farnese Gardens from the via Nova

Immediately to the right the *Clivus* meets the *via Nova*, built in the time of Nero, which was also originally part of Nero's huge arcaded entrance hall and, at a later date, part of the *porticus* of the Flavian era.

The road, only passable in certain places, is lined on both sides with rooms, mostly **shops** ⑨, that open onto the road. The better preserved ones show the remnants of paintings, mosaics, basins and counters; some of them also have space for a wooden mezzanine floor for use as a living area. Half way along the road, on the left, a modern ramp brings the visitor to the *Domus Tiberiana,* the Neronian Cryptoporticus and the Farnese Gardens. Returning back to the path, the visit continues along the *Clivus*

Palatinus, bordered on the left by the boundary wall of via di San Bonaventura and on the right by brick rooms opening onto the road, which are a continuation of the shops already seen on the corner of the *via Nova.* Continuing up the ramp, where now only the ruins of Imperial times can be seen, are some luxurious private houses of the Republican age. These were highly praised by the ancient authors for their magnificent furnishings and for their prestigious position close to the Forum, centre of the political and economic life of the city. On this gradient must have stood the house of *Lucius Licinius Crassus,* described by Pliny as "magnificent". Its entrance hall, adorned with columns of precious marbles, appeared so sumptuous that its owner was

harshly criticised and nicknamed "the Palatine Venus". Nearby, the site of the *domus* once belonging to *Marcus Livius Drusus,* tribune in 91 BC, has been identified. It is said that in order to let everybody see his sober style of life, he exhorted his architect to build his house in a style that made it possible for anyone to check up on what he was doing at any time. This house was bought by Cicero for three and half million sestertii and luxuriously converted. It was situated on the northern side of the hill, in a prominent position (*in conspectu totius urbis*). However, taking into account all the houses on the Palatine, the ancients considered the most beautiful to be that of *Marcus Aemilius Scaurus,* whose atrium had four very tall marble columns,

indeed so heavy, that during transportation much of the city's drainage system gave way under them. This house of luxury burnt down in Nero's fire, along with some age-old trees of extraordinary beauty.

Back on the right hand side of the road, there is a modern square shaped structure, lying on the ground, paved with pieces of stone that recalls one of the pillars of the **arch** ⑩. that used to cross the road at this point. The other pillar is covered by the via di San Bonaventura, as is illustrated in a drawing on the surrounding wall. There is no precise information about this construction that dates to the Domitian era. It is almost certainly an entrance archway leading to the Palace of Domitian, the facade of which is directly behind. Some interesting architectural fragments lying around probably formed part of its decoration. A little further along, again on the right hand side, where the line of shops comes to an end, is a large concrete **base** ⑪. The centre is badly broken due to the

21. Shops along the Clivus Palatinus; in the background the eastern part of the Domus Tiberiana

The inviolability of the walls and the killing of Remus

«While (Romulus and Remus) were about to found one city together, a dispute arose between them as to exactly where (...). Having decided to resolve the problem using the augurs from birds, and having set this up in different places, the story is told of six vultures appearing to Remus while the double appeared to Romulus; some believed that Remus really did see them, whereas Romulus lied, and that it was only when Remus approached that Romulus would have seen the twelve vultures (...). When Remus found out that he had been tricked, he grew angry; and as Romulus was digging a ditch which was to encompass the walls, he scoffed at his labours and tried to obstruct him. Finally he leaped the ditch

subsidence of the surrounding ground, under which runs a tight network of cuniculi and latomiae. While Lanciani considered this to be the base of a Medieval tower (*Turris Bonae Iniquitatis*), Pietro Rosa, who had found the base of tufa blocks with its archaic inscriptions, thought it was the Temple of *Juppiter Stator*, situated just outside the old city walls by the *Porta Mugonia*. The hypothesis remains an object for debate. During excavations near the base, four small archaistic columns with inscriptions were found. Three of them are currently on show in the Museo Palatino, and for some time now have been linked with the mythical quarrel between Romulus and Remus at the time of the foundation of the city.

Arriving in front of the *Domus Flavia*, at the end of the *Clivus Palatinus*, and turning to the right along the Basilica, past the House of Livia which is to the right, and the Temple of Apollo and the House of Augustus to the left, the visitor finally arrives at the summit of the *Cermalus*.

in a single bound: some say he fell there and then, others that he was struck down by Romulus himself, still others by one of his companions, a certain *Celer*» (Plutarch, *The Life of Romulus*, 9, 4 f.). It is believed that four boundary stones were dedicated to this episode of the myth regarding the founding of Rome and the struggle between Romulus and Remus. They were inscribed to *Remureine, Marspiter, Anabestas* and *Ferter Resius,* king of the *Aequiculi*, founder of the Fetials and the war law. The four boundary stones determined the limits of a sacred square area on the spot where Remus fell (hence *Remureine*) and were in memory of the sacrilege he committed by leaping across the sacred limits of the fortifications (*Anabestas* from *anabaino*, that is to say "I straddle, I mount").

22. View of the Domus Flavia from the Clivus Palatinus

THE SITE OF THE TEMPLE OF THE MAGNA MATER

On the south-western summit of the Palatine Rome's most ancient memories are to be found. Here was the ditch of Square Roma, recording the very moment of the city's foundation; here was the hut of Romulus; here the **Scalae Caci** ⑫. This stairway was one of the oldest accesses to the Palatine. According to Virgil's description, it was climbed by Aeneas together with king Evander. The name *Scalae Caci* comes from the giant Cacus, Hercules mythical opponent. The stairway was made up of alternating ramps and large steps, and was located on the hillside overlooking the Circus Maximus.

To the west of the *Scalae* protected by roofing are the bases of **three huts** ⑬. These were recorded during the Vaglieri excavations in 1907, and systematically dug in 1948. The huts can be dated to the 8th century BC, that is to say to the same period in which, according to tradition, Rome was founded, and are built on the hill's natural tufa bedrock. From the traces left on the ground of the best preserved hut, and from comparisons made with hut urns from Latium burial-grounds of the first Iron Age

(9th-8th century BC), it has been possible to make faithful reconstructions of them. A small-scale model of the huts can be seen in the Museo Palatino. The largest measured 4.90 m x 3.60 m and had seven holes along the perimeter (four at the corners, and three in intermediate positions) corresponding to the posts that sustained it. In front of the door on the shorter southern side was a small porch supported by two posts. The thatched roof was sloping, the reed walls were daubed with clay. At the centre of the hut was a hearth; outside there was a small drain to carry away the rain water.

In the area between the huts and the House of Livia are to be found two round archaic **cisterns** ⑭, in close proximity to one another. One of them, next to the atrium of Livia's House, is sunk in virgin soil, and lined with tufa blocks; a waterproof clay membrane isolates it from the natural bedrock. Its ogival cover was layered, and is of the 6th century BC. The inside was plastered and dissected by a wall of uncertain function. It seems to connect with another open air cistern of the same date not far away, that has been partially destroyed by a wall of a later date, and is only accessible by ladder.

The Lupercal

The Lupercal was the grotto sacred to the Faun Lupercus near which, according to tradition, the flood waters of the Tiber had washed ashore the basket with Romulus and Remus. The ancient writers sited this at the foot of the Palatine near the Velabrum, in the middle of a sacred wood. Inside the grotto was spring of clear water, and in front of the entrance grew the *ficus ruminalis*. Following an omen of the augur *Actus Navius* this was taken to the *Comitia* where it was still venerated in historical times. A special entrance joined the Circus Maximus with the Lupercal, where the bronze group of the she-wolf suckling was kept. From an effigy of this the oldest coins in Rome were struck.

23. Statue of the Magna Mater enthroned. Rome, Museo Palatino

24. A model reconstruction of the huts (Romulean era) on the Cermalus. Rome, Museo Palatino

Behind the huts stands the raised podium of the **Temple of the *Magna Mater*** ⑮. Nowadays it is crowned by a grove of ancient holm oaks that enhances its magic. The temple, unearthed by Pietro Rosa in the 1800s, has recently been restudied. It had a square cell raised up on a very high base and was covered with peperino blocks. It must have had six frontal columns and a wide flight of steps in front of the pronaos. This architectural reconstruction is confirmed by a relief from the first Imperial Age (presently stored in the Villa Medici, in Rome), that shows a sacred procession in front of the temple. After the fire of 111 BC, various restorations were undertaken by *Metellus Numidicus*, and in the 3rd century by order of Augustus. It is last mentioned by the historian Zosimus in the 5th century AD. Its identification is certified by some inscriptions, and by the recovery of a statue of the seated goddess, now on view in the Museo Palatino. On the day of dedication in 191 BC, the *Ludi Megalenses* were performed. They took place on a platform in front of the pronaos, on a terrace still visible today, that was supported by walls made from parallel tufa blocks and datable to the 3rd century BC. At a later date, the selfsame structures were reused to build a series of rooms, perhaps shops, that opened onto an internal covered road that ran through the complex. Recent excavations to the east of the Temple of the *Magna Mater* have uncovered the foundations and remains of a podium of a large temple built in square tufa blocks (*opus quadratum*). In the same area, inside the *favissae*, the sacred ditches, two very beautiful terracotta heads have been found, probably from the fronton, as well as slabs and polychrome earthware facings, now exhibited in the Museo Palatino. The building has been identified as the **Temple of Victory**, built in 294 BC by the consul *Lucius*

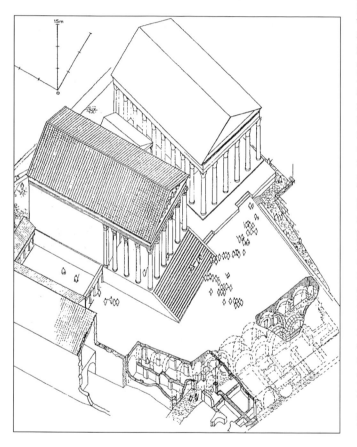

25. Assonometrical reconstruction of the Temple of the Magna Mater and the Temple of Victory

The *Lupercalia*

The so-called *Lupercalia* or *Lupercale sacrum* feasts were established, according to tradition, by Romulus and Remus. They were celebrated each year on 15 February for the purpose of purifying shepherds and their flocks following the sacrifice of kid goats, special prayers of expiation. Two youths were selected, their foreheads were touched with the blade of the knife still dripping with blood, and afterwards this was wiped clean with wool soaked in milk. After the sacred banquet the priests wrapped in ox leather ran round the perimeter of the city armed with branches of twigs. The married women of Rome allowed themselves to be beaten in the hope that they would be made pure and fertile (Ovid, *Fasti*, II, 267 and fol.)

Postumius Megellus and to which, in 193 BC, *Marcus Porcius Cato* added a shrine dedicated to the *Victoria Virgo*. This last piece of information has made many scholars believe that the small brick construction between the Temple of the *Magna Mater* and the Temple of Victory, traditionally identified with the **Auguratorium** ⑯ (the place where the augurs observed the flight of birds to make auspices, mentioned only in the Catalogues) could in fact be the sacellum of the *Victoria Virgo*. However, with the discovery on site of some antefixes with the head of

Juno Sospita, scholars are nowadays more inclined to identify the small building as the temple of this latter goddess, which Ovid mentions as being close to the Temple of the *Magna Mater*. From the summit, where the hill drops down to the Circus Maximus and the *Velabrum*, in

the south-western corner of the hill, hidden among the many multistoried **brick structures** ⑰ (identified as some of the 89 domus and the 2742 *insulae* mentioned in the Regionary Catalogues), there are the remains of some **walls** ⑱ of tufa blocks that once fortified this side of the hill.

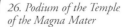

26. Podium of the Temple of the Magna Mater

27. Head of a divinity crowned with vine leaves (beginning of the 3rd century BC), from the site of the Temple of Victory. Rome, Museo Palatino

THE HOUSE OF AUGUSTUS, THE TEMPLE OF APOLLO AND THE HOUSE OF LIVIA

The house that Augustus had purchased on the Palatine from the orator Hortensius was so modest, that after the victory of Naulochos (36 BC), the Senate decided to build him a new house with public money on the land he had bought and declared it State property. Furthermore, the Senate was so grateful to him for having put an end to the civil wars, that it conferred on Octavian the title of Augustus, and planted two laurel trees at the entrance with a civic crown above the gate.

In the fire of the 3rd century AD the house was badly destroyed and many offered considerable amounts of money for its restoration. According to Cassius Dio, Augustus symbolically accepted an *aureus* from the community and a *denarius* from private funds. In the public part of his house he dedicated the Temple of Apollo that was joined to the Portico of the Danaids and the Libraries. Soon after his election as *Pontifex Maximus* (12 BC), he also consecrated an altar as well as a statue of Vesta.

The excavations begun in the '60s have allowed scholars to precisely identify the Augustan complex, the Temple of Apollo and the **House of Livia** ⑲.

This latter dwelling had already been excavated by Pietro Rosa in 1869.
The house, previously thought to be that of Germanicus, was attributed to Livia, Augustus' wife, after the discovery of some led pipes with the inscription *Iulia Augusta*.
The house lies at a lower level than the surrounding buildings, and entrance is gained by means of a descending corridor (A). The floor of this corridor is of black and white mosaic and leads into a covered atrium, with two pillars supporting the roof (B). The back of the atrium gives onto three parallel rooms of which that in the centre, the tablinum (C), is the largest compared to the lateral ones (D, E). On the right hand side of the atrium (F) is the triclinium.

It is still not clear whether the access corridor belongs to a later period, as it brings the visitor in at the back of the house. The *domus* can be dated to the 1st century BC, but with at least two subsequent phases: in fact, the masonry in *opus reticulatum* – small and somewhat irregular – dates to the beginning of the 1st century BC, whereas the pictorial decoration in the Second Style belongs to a subsequent phase, around 30 BC. When the frescos were detached from the walls, and put again *in situ* on wooden supports, it was noticed that the plaster also covered the doors which had previously been blocked up. The tablinum is the most important space as far as paintings are concerned, even

28. House of Augustus. Frescos from "the room of masks"

29. Livia's House. The right wing: detail of the painted decoration of rich floral garlands

though the frescoes are so faded that they do not allow for a complete reading of the scenes depicted.

The wall on the right is divided into three parts by a portico of Corinthian columns standing on high plinths. In the largest and most important central niche is depicted Io, beloved by Jupiter. In the scene, Mercury is freeing her from her imprisonment by Argus into which the very jealous Juno had led her. The black haired girl is sitting at the foot of a column that supports a statue. On the right is Argus, the armed gaoler, while Mercury, the liberator, is approaching from the left. The scene, also to be found in Pompeian painting, derives from a famous work of the 4th century BC by the Athenian painter Nicias. Also depicted is an open window, with a prospective view onto a city street animated by various scenes of people at the windows of the houses.

The nymph Galatea is shown in the central panel on the back wall. She is depicted on a sea horse galloping away from Polyphemus, who, driven by a cupid is longingly advancing towards her, with his enormous body immersed in the waves; Mount Etna is seen in the distance. Sphinxes, candelabra, winged gods and racemes, enrich the architectural motifs. On the left hand wall the plaster crumbled a long time ago. In the left wing, the decoration is made up of columns and pillars standing on plinths of fake marble. On the back wall, winged griffins and elegantly stylised figures are depicted in pastel colours on a white background: these are the

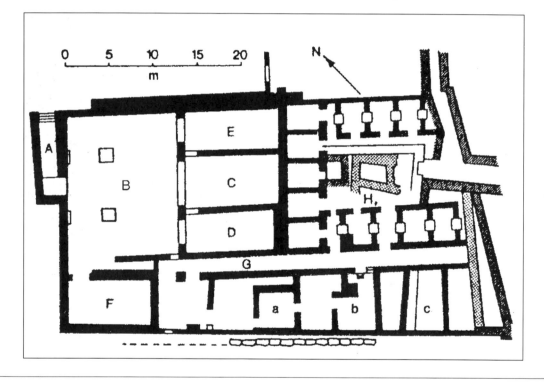

30. Plan of Livia's House
A. Back entrance
B. Courtyard
C. Tablinum
D-E. Wings
F. Triclinium
G. Corridor
H. Atrium area?
a. b. c. Upper floor rooms

31. Livia's House.
Left wing, detail of the
painted decoration with
fantastic figures facing
each other on candelabra

figures that Vitruvius scoffed at as being too fanciful and unreal.

In the right wing, the back wall is missing: on the side walls is depicted a portico of Corinthian columns with luxuriant garlands of leaves, flowers and fruits, tied up with gaily coloured ribbons, and hanging rural cult objects; a yellow frieze runs along the top. This work is regarded as one of the most important examples of Roman landscape painting. Human beings, animals, exotic buildings, shrines, ritual scenes follow one another uninterruptedly in an admirable impressionistic style. The triclinium also shows a pictorial decoration using fake architectural motifs, such as open windows, that were themes particularly dear to the Romans, especially when there were no gardens at hand. On the long wall to the left, the most important of all, is a semi-circular portico with statues on its attic. Opposite can be seen a rustic trophy with the hides of animals and other symbols dear to the goddess Diana. For the most part the mosaic floors are well preserved. They have a black and white tesserae motif, woven like a rug, with a band all around and the occasional design in the centre.

The hypothesis that Livia's House although only part of Augustus' house, was her domain and hers alone, is nowadays accepted by the majority of scholars.

The House of Augustus was really a complex, made up of a number of existing houses. Velleius Paterculus recounts that Octavian, after his victory over Sextus Pompey

(36 BC), "purchased through an intermediary several houses in order to enlarge his own" (2, 81).

The **House of Augustus** ⑳, closely adjoining the nearby Temple of Apollo, consists of a series of rooms on two levels of the hill facing the Circus Maximus. On the lower terrace the excavated rooms, built of square tufa blocks (*opus quadratum*) laid out in two lines, lean up against a strongly robust wall in *opus caementicium*, built to retain the ground above. The simplicity and modest dimensions of the rooms perfectly fit the description given by Suetonius: "(a house) neither agreeable for its luxury nor for its comfort, as there were only small peperino columned porches and rooms without any decorative marbles or patterned floors" (*Augustus*, 72, 1-2).

The house, restored by Augustus after the fire of 3 AD, had a private side, with small modest rooms, as well as a public side – closer to the Temple of Apollo – with wider and more elegant rooms, that were embellished with stucco ceilings and marble floors. It is from this house that the most important series of wall paintings of the Second Style have been recovered in recent years. In the private sector the most significant discoveries to be found were in two small adjoining rooms: "the mask room" (room 5) and "the room with pine garlands" (room 6). The former displays a rich architectural decoration inspired by theatrical scenographies, to which the masks on the cornice also refer. In the centre of each wall a rural sanctuary is depicted. The second room has a decorative layout similar to that of Pompeian houses: pine garlands are strewn among the wooden pilasters of a porch that stands on a high podium. The public part of the house has a more organic architectural approach to it. Even the painting shows a greater formal care. The "black walled" room (room 7) is divided into panels using bright red pilaster strips with yellow borders at the corners. The so-called "Western Library" (room 8) has niches in the walls, and the painted

32. Livia's House. The right wing: detail of the yellow frieze, with landscape scenes

33. House of Augustus. Detail of the painted decoration in the "Studiolo"

decoration is divided into two parts: in the entrance, on the left, large yellow panels stand out against the red background; in the interior, the red background is bordered by green and yellow bands.

In the two subsequent rooms (rooms 9-10) the decoration is not so well preserved. It is much simpler and the predominant colours are green, yellow and red. In the so-called "room of perspectives" (room 11), a two storey building has been projected forward giving rise to a complex perspective effect. Parts of the lacunar ceiling are still intact. On the ramp that leads from the house to the Temple of Apollo, of considerable height, light hues alternate with darker ones. On the southern wall the decoration is divided into two parts. The theme is the standard one of a projecting podium surmounted by pillars. High up on the back wall is a view of some buildings with windows. The vault has painted lacunars. The left wall of the ramp is much better preserved and consists of simple rows of blocks, a pictorial image of the walls in *opus reticulatum*.

The large colonnaded room (room 13) has inlaid marble floor and stuccoed vaulting while the pictorial decoration is broadly conceived. Above the socle the tripartite architectural composition is enriched by paintings of figures and masks. The multicoloured frieze with vegetal decorations on a black background is very refined. The little square room (room 14) has an inlaid marble floor; in the pictorial decoration, above the podium, the walls are divided by purple panels and depict the external world, made up of figures and genre scenes. However, the room that surpasses all others in the refinement and variety of its pictorial motifs is unquestionably the upper cubicle, also referred to as "Augustus' Studiolo" (room 15). This has been reassembled thanks to a long and accurate work of restoration. The vividness of its colours and the eloquence of its design is quite extraordinary. The decorative form is the usual: a podium,

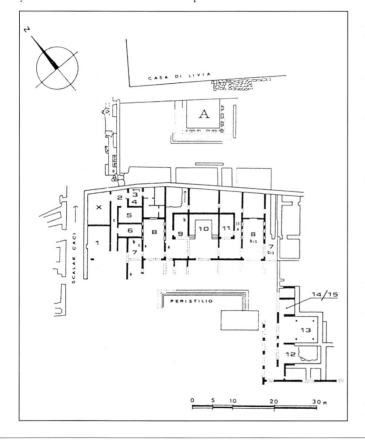

34. Ground plan of the House of Augustus
1-6. Private rooms
7-14. Public rooms
5. "The Room of Masks"
6. "The Room of Pine Garlands"
7. "The Black Walled Room"
8. "The Western Library"
11. "The Room of Perspectives"
12. Access Ramp to the Temple of Apollo
13. Colonnaded Hall
14. Small square room
15. The "Studiolo"

orthostats and upper zone, where the prevailing colours are the standard ones: red, yellow and black. The most original part of the decoration is represented by panels with figures alongside friezes and small decorated squares. Details are very carefully handled and often repeated; swans, calyces, winged griffins, candelabra, lotus flowers, all motifs of clear Alexandrine derivation. The magnificent ceiling has finely alternating stucco-work and painted panels.

Adjoining, and closely connected to the eastern side of the house, stands the **Temple of Apollo** ㉑, one of the most important buildings on the Palatine and indeed of the whole of Augustan architecture. For its solemn dedication in 28 BC, both Horace and Propertius wrote poems. Ovid and Virgil also mention it in their works. Initially excavated by Pietro Rosa, who thought it to be the Temple of Jupiter the Victorious, it has only recently been correctly identified. The whole structure was built of white marble from Luni and its doors were gilded and inlaid with ivory. It was surrounded by a colonnaded portico of *giallo antico*, which was adorned in between the columns with fifty statues of the Danaids, the unfortunate daughters of Danaus, king of

35. House of Augustus. Fresco and stucco decoration on the ceiling of the "Studiolo"

Egypt. There were statues of Apollo, Latona and Artemis, respectively by Skopas, Kephisodotos the Younger and Timotheos, expressly brought from Greece to embellish the interior. The Sybilline Books were kept in the base of Apollo's statue, while other works of art were stored in the Libraries. Nowadays the temple appears totally stripped: all that remains is the nucleous of the podium in *opus caementicium* (44 m x 24 m) and a few fragments of what must have been a very rich marble decoration. The colossal statue of Apollo is in a similar condition for only bits and pieces of it remain. The two most important of these are a part of the face and a part of the foot, which are now in the Museo Palatino. Several beautifully worked polychrome terracotta slabs were recovered during excavations. The slabs represent sacred and mythical themes related to the cult of Apollo, selected to express the rich ideological significance of the political programme launched by Augustus after the battle of Actium. The so-called "portico of the Danaids" must almost certainly have been decorated with them, as they were strictly connected with the temple. Recently, three of the Danaids that adorned the homonymous portico have been identified. They are the three hermae in Greek black marble (*nero antico*), excavated by Pietro Rosa near the base of the temple. Together with the hermae other important sculptures were found, now exhibited in the Museo Palatino. These included, among others, the ephebe in basalt, a portrait of Nero, and another one of a veiled young Julio-Claudian prince (perhaps Nero as a youth).

36. Fresco of Apollo the Citharist, from the site of the House of Augustus. Rome, Museo Palatino

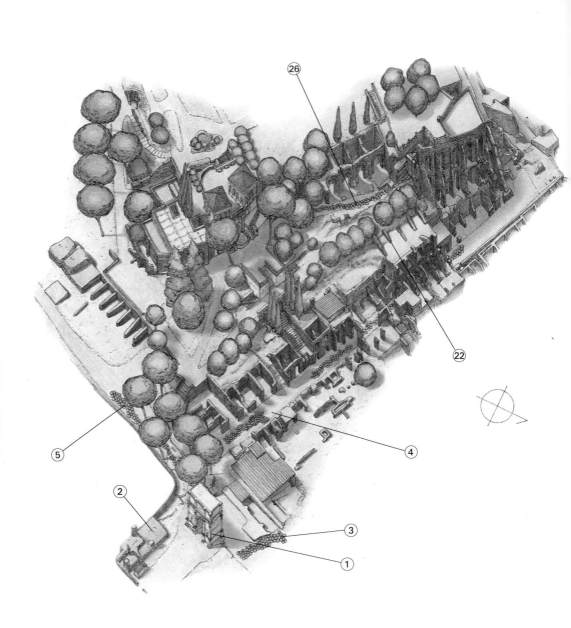

1 Arch of Titus
2 Base
3 *via Sacra*
4 *via Nova*
5 *Clivus Palatinus*
22 *Domus Tiberiana*
26 Victory *Clivus*

THE DOMUS TIBERIANA

The **Domus Tiberiana** ㉒ stands in the north-western corner of the hill. With its imposing arcades it offers a theatrical backdrop to the forum. It is the first of the imperial palaces on the Palatine conceived in an organic and monumental manner.

Although ancient sources do not attribute to Tiberius the building of an imperial residence, we know that his house, later owned by Germanicus, was on the Palatine. Statius tells us that before becoming emperor Claudius also, lived in Tiberius' house. The location of the Palace is confirmed in a passage by Suetonius (*Galba*, I, 8) and also by Plutarch (*Life of Galba*, 18, 1), both of whom suggest that the building was on the side of the Palatine facing the Capitol and the Forum. It must be remembered, however, that the *Domus Tiberiana* is only mentioned for the first time in a description of the riots of 69 AD. The building extended over an area of approximately 150 m x 120 m, to which must be added the extension carried out by Caligula in the direction of the Forum and those by Domitian in the direction of the *Clivus Palatinus*. The remains of the *Domus* are imposing, especially those on the northern side, which have been well preserved to a height of nearly twenty metres. They are, however, nothing in comparison to its original splendour. Today only the lower floors remain, the piano nobile of the original buildings was destroyed and is now covered by the Farnese Gardens. During the 1st century AD the Palace was seriously damaged by two terrible fires: that of 64 AD and that of 80 AD. Following the latter, Domitian rebuilt the facade facing the Forum, adding a long loggia to the new front and remodelling the *Domus* into a sort of giant appendix to the great Palace which he had built on the summit of the hill.

It was Trajan, but above all Hadrian, who continued the building works. The latter built the large arcades spanning the Victory *Clivus* and brought the facade of the Palace right up to the *via Nova*, with a truly spectacular architectural feat.

Under Commodus, the *Domus* was again consumed by fire. This time it destroyed the important library, in which the imperial archives were kept. Several passages of the late authors mention that the *Domus Tiberiana* was particularly loved by the Antonine emperors.

Even in the 8th century AD it was used as the residence of Pope John VII, son of Plato, *curator* of the Imperial Palaces.

Abandoned and looted during the Middle Ages, what remained of Tiberius' Palace in the middle of the 1500 was eventually buried under the Farnese Gardens. The *Domus Tiberiana* was excavated for the first time in the 1800s by Pietro Rosa, who uncovered the northern facade facing the Forum. He also excavated the eastern facade up to the Cryptoporticus, that once connected the Palace with the *Domus Flavia*, and finally the southern one facing the Temple of the *Magna Mater*. Recent excavations have shown that, despite appearances, the *Domus Tiberiana* is not an organic, uniform building, neither architecturally nor chronologically, but a complex progressively formed over the years and by a train of events. Initially, as with

---

The Farnese Gardens

Descending from the Barberini Vineyard, back onto the *Clivus Palatinus*, it is not difficult to reach the terrace of the Farnese Gardens, last on our itinerary. The *Horti Palatini Farnesiorum*, as reads the inscription over Vignola's portal, were created in the middle of the 16th century by Cardinal Alessandro Farnese, nephew to Pope Paul III. Designed by Vignola with great scenographical effect, they stretched from the Forum to the summit of the hill. Vignola's plans were executed by Gerolamo Rainaldi at the beginning of the 17th century. From the entrance portal to the Forum (now reassembled in via di San Gregorio) the visitor reached the first terrace (nowadays by stairway from the *via Nova*). After passing a small portico with seats, the visitor comes to the Nymphaeum of Rain. This is a large hall with the vaults and walls covered with paintings (today in a bad state of decay). The frescos show some people leaning over a balustrade under a pergola of vines, a motif dear to artists of the Renaissance. At the back stands a large fountain of

Augustus' House, it was made up of a series of separate *domus* of the Late-Republican age. Remains of Republican houses that covered this part of the hill, have been found in abundance in the course of excavations. In the time of Nero the *domus* were contained and enclosed by a base consisting of a strong perimetrical wall, reinforced by buttresses. It was only then that the real Palace was born and although it bore the name of Tiberius, was in fact built by Nero.

Such dating, if confirmed, would suggest that the *Domus Tiberiana* is but a single element of the grandiose complex, built after 64 AD, that stretched from the Palatine as far as the Esquiline, and was for a very good reason called the *Domus Aurea*.

It is advisable to start the visit from the southern side, opposite the Temple of the *Magna Mater*. Here are to be found a series of eighteen **brick rooms** ㉔, from the time of Nero. Remains of paintings from the 3rd

stalactites. From this level the Theatre of the Great Fountain (the "*Fontanone*") with its central niche is reached, by way of ramps. To go to the upper terrace there are two stairways which both have niches decorated with stucco work. At this point the visitor enters the main gardens. At the summit

Rainaldi built two arcaded pavilions with pagoda-like roofs to be used as Aviaries. These were restored to their original condition (apart from the roofs) in the '50s. On the eastern side of the Gardens, towards the *Clivus Palatinus*, is an apsed fountain called the Nymphaeum of Mirrors,

engraved with the lily of the Farnese coat of arms. The niches and walls are covered with mosaics and stalactites. Above the Nymphaeum, in an enclosure planted with trees, with the Fountain of the Plane-trees at its centre, meetings of the *Academia of Arcadia* used to be held towards the end

of the 17th century. Very little remains of the original Farnese Gardens. The neatly arranged gardens of today, planted with rare trees and flower beds are from the 19th century and were designed by Pietro Rosa, who lived there, and Giacomo Boni who was buried in the flower garden close to the Aviaries.

century AD can still be seen in the vaults, although they are practically illegible nowadays. Still legible, however, are the graffiti on the plastered walls, they suggest that these rooms were logistical support quarters, perhaps those of the guard. In front of them Pietro Rosa found the very beautiful statue of the *Charis*, now in the Museo Palatino.

In the south-eastern corner of the Palace, by the gardens, opposite Livia's House, stands a large elliptic **basin** ㉕ with wide steps on the inside, that may well have been a fishpond. Continuing along the eastern side of the Palace the visitor comes upon the fascinating **Neronian Cryptoporticus** ㉓, 130 meters in length and lit by windows. The poorly preserved plaster on the walls is decorated with geometrical motifs, and the floor is paved with mosaics.

A transversal arm from a later period, connected Tiberius' Palace with the *Domus Flavia*. At the beginning of the vault to the cryptoporticus, close to Livia's House, there is a copy of the original stucco decoration, with geometrical panels and scenes of cupids entwined in vegetal motifs. Outside the Cryptoporticus, leaving behind Domitian's extensions on the left, the

visitor arrives at the Palace's northern side, which is most imposing and important with its arcaded facade facing the Forum. It is all built around an internal road called the **Victory *Clivus*** ㉖. On the left hand side, further along this road, are the front rooms of Domitian's facade to the Palace, enclosed by an open gallery, supported by travertine corbels and bordered by a marble transenna. Worth noting is the very refined stucco coating on the underside of the vaults. The internal rooms, poorly lit due to the projecting facade facing the

Forum, are decorated with stucco-work and wall paintings of the Flavian era. Some of the graffiti can be discerned in several of the downstairs rooms: lascivious writing, lists of calculations and play boards, probably scribbled by the guards. Further along on the left is a long and ancient stairway inlaid with marble. In older times it led to the Palace's piano nobile, but now goes up to the Farnese Gardens. The large arcades spanning the street, and the rooms to the right, of a different orientation to that of the Palace, were built by

37. View of the Domus Tiberiana from the Roman Forum

38. The Domus Tiberiana. Southern prospect facing the Temple of the Magna Mater

The cult of *Febris*

The unhealthy conditions of the plains around the Palatine, induced the Romans of the Archaic periods to dedicate a *fanum* or temple (with an altar inside) to *Febris*, the personification of fever. The altar was surrounded by a small square, and

was most likely built on the slopes of the hill towards the Velabrum. Many authors agree that the cult was important and that it continued until the Late Empire.

Tiberius' Palace directly with the Forum.

To conclude the visit to the *Domus Tiberiana* it is better to go up to the level of the gardens, where the real Palace, now destroyed, once stood. Recent excavations on the terrace have shown that the present layout of the area as a garden, supplants one that actually once existed. More precisely, in the time of Nero, this level had built up areas alternating with green ones, according to a plan that scholars have been able to reconstruct. This shows a central building surrounded by gardens, with pavilions on each of the four sides. Excavations have shown that even after Nero, that is to say

Hadrian. He had the front of the Palace moved forward with the result that the road was blocked within the complex and became a *via tecta*.
All the most important material found in the *Domus* comes from these rooms. During excavations in the 1800s, two altars dedicated to Minerva and Lucina were discovered, together with a beautiful head of a dying Persian. Recently high quality fragments of terracotta statues have been found. They were probably exemplars of *proplasmata*, the clay models from which the

sculptors *Pasiteles, Stephanos* and *Arkesilaos*, reproduced those Greek masterpieces most requested by wealthy Romans in the time between Caesar and Augustus.
Where the *Clivus* turns to the left, and from a platform with a good view over the Forum below, the visitor can see the imposing halls, with their well preserved high walls, built by Domitian on the remains of Caligula's House (**Atrium Gai**) ㉗.
From the *clivus*, they are reached by way of an impressive covered ramp, dating from the time of Domitian, that connected

The Death of Caligula

One of the cryptoportici in the *Domus Tiberiana* (we do not know precisely which one) was the scenario for Caligula's dramatic assassination. It came about after a plot had been hatched by the two tribunes *Cornelius*

Sabinus and *Cassius Chaerea*. Suetonius narrates (*Gaius*, 58) that on 24 January AD 41 Caligula, who was suffering from stomach pains, was advised by his friends to go for a walk along the cryptoporticus. When he stopped to chat with some young nobles

who had arrived from Asia for a performance, *Sabinus*, *Chaerea* and others fell upon him and stabbed him thirty times.

under Domitian and Hadrian, the 'green' layout continued to be an architectural characteristic of the site. Moreover, the existence of gardens in Tiberius' Palace is confirmed by written sources of the Julio-Claudian era: for example Suetonius relates that after Caligula's murder, Claudius in order to escape the conspirators "sheltered in a *diaeta* called *Hermaeum*; after a while terrified by the noise, he hid himself in the nearby *solarium*" (*Claudius*, 10). In Caligula's time therefore, the Palace already had a *diaeta* (a pavilion) and a *solarium* (a terrace), two elements which are usually connected with green areas. Perhaps the Farnese knew that this particular site had been used for hanging gardens since antiquity, and keeping to ancient topography, as was their ideal, decided to establish their own gardens precisely on this terrace.

39. *Terracotta head of Apollo from the Domus Tiberiana. Rome, Palazzo Massimo alle Terme*

40. *Statue of the so-called Charis from the southern side of the Domus Tiberiana. Rome, Museo Palatino*

41. *Domus Tiberiana. Northern prospect looking on to the Victory Clivus*

42. *Terracotta Apollonian head from the Domus Tiberiana. Rome, Palazzo Massimo alle Terme*

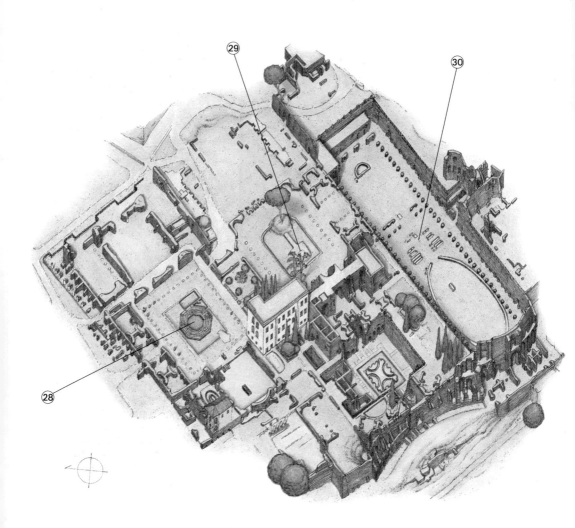

㉘ *Domus Flavia*
㉙ *Domus Augustana*
㉚ Stadio

THE PALACE OF THE FLAVIANS: THE DOMUS FLAVIA, THE DOMUS AUGUSTANA AND THE STADIUM

Back on the Victory *Clivus*, past the large Farnese Fountain, and across the little verdant valley shaded by large cedars, the visitor arrives in front of the *Domus Flavia,* which occupies the highest and most central part of the Palatine. Commissioned by Domitian (81-96 AD) and built by the architect Rabirius, it filled the depression between the *Palatium* and the *Cermalus*. It was built on top of former buildings, some of which (the House of the Griffins, the *Aula Isiaca* and the *Domus Transitoria)* are still visible beneath it to this day.
The Palace can be divided into three parts: the *Domus Flavia*, the public part and entertainment area (to the west); the *Domus Augustana,* the residential area and private domain of the emperor (in the centre); and the *Stadium,* (to the east).
It was built entirely in brick, and what remains today still gives the visitor an idea of the grandeur of its proportions, of the technical skill of its builders, and of the planimetric variety of its construction. This is especially so in the private areas, where it must have been easier to get away from traditional architectural design. The Palace created a great sensation, as the chroniclers of that time report, especially Statius, Martial and Plutarch, whose descriptions praise the refinement of the decoration of the building; such as the polychrome marble used in the columns, the veneer on the floors and walls, and the splendid stucco-work on the vaulted ceilings.
Martial, in particular, describes the Palace as "one of the most beautiful things in the world, a high colossal mass, as if seven mountains rose one above the other, to touch the sky, to which it alone was equal, but still so much less than the lord that dwelt within" (*Epigrams*, VIII, 36).
Despite the plunder of the Middle Ages, excavations have confirmed the truth of those ancient descriptions. The historian Flaminio Vacca recounts that the threshold to the Central Hall of the *Domus Flavia* was made from a single block of Greek marble that had to be cut for the great altar of the *Pantheon,* for which it was difficult to find a single slab that was large enough. Domitian's Palace represents a milestone in the history of Roman architecture, because it exemplifies the style of construction of Roman dynastic palaces, with the private domain strictly separated from the public one. The function of apses, found in many public halls, was in fact to separate the emperor from the thronging masses. The visit can start at the **Domus Flavia** ㉘. The facade opens onto a portico of cipolin marble columns, divided into three foreparts, corresponding to the three interior halls. The same portico is also found on the western side. Along the facade the structure takes on the form of a covered terrace from which the emperor would appear to the people. It led into three vast back halls, used for official ceremonies. The first hall on the left, smaller than the others, was

43. F. Dutert (1845-1905). Reconstructed section of the Domus Flavia showing the Lararium, the Aula Regia and the "Basilica" (1871)

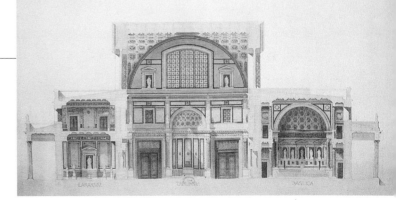

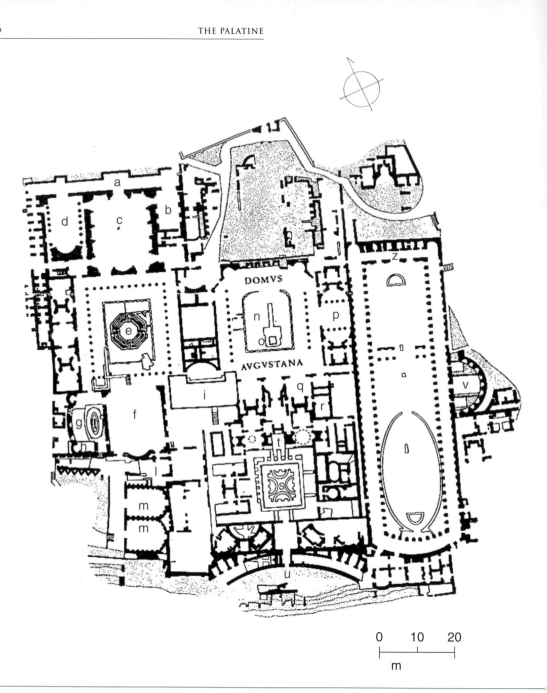

44. Plan of the Flavians Palace

a   Portico
b   Lararium
c   Aula regia
d   Basilica
e   Peristyle
f   Triclinium
g   Nymphaeum
h   Farnese Lodge
i   Museo Palatino

l   "Academia"
m   Libraries
n   Colonnaded Peristyle
o   Little Temple
p   Porticoed Diaeta
q   Oratory of San Cesareo
r   Loggia Mattei
s   Peristyle

t   Living areas
u   Colonnaded Exhedra
v   Imperial Box
z   Logistical support spaces

called the *Lararium*: the presence of a structure at the back, has been unconvincingly interpreted as an altar, and therefore was considered to be the emperor's private chapel.

At the centre was the largest room (30.50 m x 38.70 m) called the *Aula Regia* (Audience Chamber) by archaeologists of the 1700s. It had *pavonazzetto* marble columns standing against the walls which were veneered in polychrome marbles, and niches for the statues. Given the ample dimensions of this hall and the subtlety of its structure, it was unlikely to have had a vaulted ceiling, even though many of the reconstruction drawings might show it as such.

The apse is at the back; next to it is a plaque to commemorate the excavations of the 1700s carried out by Francis I of Parma. In the apse the throne of the emperor, *dominus et deus*, once stood. It was in this hall that he gave audience, received ambassadors and presided over meetings. On the walls can be seen many architectural fragments of the original decorations. Two colossal statues in basalt, representing Hercules and Apollo, recovered during the excavations of the 1700s, are today in Parma, where they

45. *Domus Flavia. Northern Prospect*

46. *Domus Flavia. The octagonal fountain of the upper peristyle*

47. *Domus Flavia. Triclinium*

were taken after F. Bianchini's excavations.

Because of its size and wealth of architectural and sculptural decorations, the Hall can truly be considered one of the most magnificent expressions of Flavian baroque.

The third hall on the right, called the Basilica, is rectangular in shape, and has three aisles and columns of *giallo antico*. At the back is the apse, closed off by a marble transenna. On the floor is a semicircular marble gutter and there are two skylights corresponding to the cistern below, dating from the time of Nero.

The presence of an apse in the room indicates that this was where ceremonies were held presided over by the emperor. Until recently, the room was thought to have been used for judicial hearings, now however, it has been suggested that it might well have been the *Auditorium*, and used for political and administrative consultations.

Beyond these rooms, to the south, stretched the spacious peristyle, surrounded by a colonnaded portico of *portasanta* marble, with an octagonal impluvium in the form of a fountain at the centre. It was here that Domitian used to stroll beneath the porticoes that went by the name of "Sicily".

Constantly suspicious, and in fear of being attacked, he had the walls veneered with slabs of shining marble from Cappadocia so that images were reflected and he could watch his back.

To the south of the peristyle, past a line of pillars of which only the bases remain, the visitor arrives at a large square hall with an apse in the rear. This is the Triclinium, the famous *Coenatio Iovis*

mentioned in ancient texts. It is paved with different coloured marbles, which are still conserved in the exhedra. In this Banquet Hall was to be found the emperor's table, raised up one step, so that he could stay clear of the crowds. It was here that the famous *ambrosiae dapes* and the *palatinae mensae* took place, during which refined dishes were consumed and nectar was drunk, while the guests

*48. Domus Flavia.
Western Nymphaeum*

enjoyed views of the extensive gardens of the peristyle, which echoed to the sound of the waters playing in the fountains.

The Triclinium was one of the most sumptuous rooms of the Palace. In the following extract Domitian's ostentation is harshly criticised by Plutarch: «You are neither pious nor charitable of heart, you are simply a manic who enjoys squandering his wealth building houses and wishing, like the famous king Midas, that everything you own turns to gold or precious stones» (*Life of Publichola*, 15, 5f.). Symmetrically placed on either side of the Triclinium, and visible from the spacious windows, were two elliptical Nymphaei, one of which is very well preserved. These were marble paved rectangular basins out of which rose an oval fountain with its niches soaked by the spewing waters. The Renaissance building behind the Nymphaeum, is all that remains of the Farnese Lodge, with its painted double loggia attributed to the Zuccari school, dated from the middle of the 1500s. At the opposite corner stands the Museo Palatino (the structure is from the 1800s), which has now reopened to visitors.

From the back of the Triclinium, through two openings, one on either side of the apse, it is possible to

49. Domus Flavia.
The so-called "Academia"

50. Domus Augustana.
Lower peristyle

reach the buildings beyond: a row of columns, once part of a portico, interpreted by Rosa as the *Academia*, as well as two parallel apsed rooms, probably belonging to the Libraries, that Domitian had built following the destruction of the ones in the House of Augustus.

To the east of the *Domus Flavia*, and adjacent to it, was the **Domus Augustana** ㉙, the private residence of the emperor. Compared with the public side with its few vast reception halls, the private quarters of the house, for the sake of variety, had spacious rooms alternating with very small ones, all built around peristyles. The building was on two floors: the upper floor was at the same level as the *Domus Flavia*, the lower one, about 12 metres below. The upper floor was arranged around a large colonnaded peristyle (of the columns only the plinths remain) with a stretch of water in the middle to brighten things up. In the

pool stood a small temple on an high podium, that could be reached by crossing a little bridge, which was supported by arches, and perhaps dedicated to Minerva, the goddess so dear to Domitian. The Corinthian columns were of *giallo antico* and *pavonazzetto*. At the sides of the peristyle and in communication with it, Alfonso Bartoli's excavations located many rooms with mixtilinear plans, among which was a large hall with two apses (perhaps a porticoed *diaeta*) and some water basins. All of these elements together give this part of the *Domus Augustana* an idyllic sacral quality, with the garden extending – in conformity with Hellenistic taste – to fill the whole area between the little temple and the surrounding buildings. The northern end of the peristyle is sadly lacking. All that can be inferred is that it was a vast open space. It had a floor of *bipedales*, and

perhaps an entrance hall for access to the Palace. Towards the south following the demolition of the Villa Mills, decided by both Giacomo Boni and Alfonso Bartoli, the ancient planimetry has been recovered. To the rear of the peristyle, a colonnaded entrance leads into a semicircular hall. All around are symmetrically grouped rooms (cubicles, rooms, baths) separated by corridors. In one of these rooms Bartoli discovered traces of Christian paintings, that are now no longer visible. He attributed these to the Oratory of San Cesareo, that took over the Palace in late Antiquity. Another of the rooms around the upper peristyle – where the paintings from the *Aula Isiaca* are currently on show – was converted into the *Loggia Mattei*, which remains a precious testimony to the Renaissance layout of the hill. Built on columns, it was moved indoors in 1595, when the owners, the Mattei, covered the court with a vaulted ceiling. The pictorial decorations, in the past considered Raphael's work, have now been attributed to Peruzzi's circle, and dated around 1520. Thanks to the recent restoration, it has been possible to replace the tondos depicting the signs of the zodiac to their original setting. In recent years they

51. Domus Augustana. Upper peristyle

52. General view of the vault of the Loggia Mattei

beds, shrubs and sculptures, that gave a certain dynamism to the central fountain. The outdoor area was surrounded by living areas and nymphaei, that on hot summer days made this part of the Palace a particularly pleasant place to be. To the north, against the rock of the hillside, there are three spacious halls, interesting examples of mixtilinear architecture. The central hall has two apses, the lateral ones show an octagonal plan and an open cupola. The facade facing the Circus Maximus had a grand colonnaded exhedra. On this side there are also some rooms with strange mixtilinear architecture, which have niches and curved walls, perhaps porticoed *dietae* intended for repose and meditation. The lower floor of the *Domus Augustana* is perhaps the most fascinating of the whole Palace, both for its rich and well designed architecture as

were given back by the Metropolitan Museum of New York. The murals, instead, are still stored in the Hermitage Museum in Saint Petersburg. From this side of the Palace, the lower floor (presently closed to the public) can be seen some ten metres below. Access is gained by means of an ancient stairway behind the Museo Palatino. Descending and skirting a narrow arcaded courtyard, regarded as the prototype for Italian Renaissance courts, the visitor goes through a long corridor, before coming to the heart of the building. This is a large

peristyle, once with porticoes of two stories but nowadays despoiled of all its veneers and decorations. A large fountain stood in the centre with motifs of *peltae* (curvilinear Amazonian shields). The pool was set in the midst of flower

*53. Overall view
of the Stadium*

*54. The Stadium.
Northern prospect*

The Hippodromes of the Roman world are in fact derivations of Greek gymnasiums and must be regarded as garden areas. The Hippodrome on the Palatine was surrounded by a wide ringed avenue from which secondary pathways and flower beds branched off. The area designed for walking was conceived as in a perspective, a panoramic route where the decorative vegetal element was important. It was common practice for it to be covered on foot, by litter or even by carriage, as both Martial and Juvenal have testified. Often these hippodromes were furnished as true and proper art galleries, rich in all types of marbles. Under this regard the Palatine Stadium was no exception. In fact most of the sculptures exhibited in the Museo Palatino come from here. Shafts of granite and cipolin marble columns lay scattered about on the ground, along with capitals and architectural fragments of the original richly decorated marbles.

The *Viridarium* too, was probably to be found in the Stadium. It is mentioned as existing inside imperial palaces, and we know for certain that in summer the Emperor Heliogabalus had a mountain of snow carried inside one.

well as for its almost timeless cosy atmosphere.

To the east of the private quarters lies the Palatine **Stadium** or Hippodrome ③⓪. The best place to view this is from the top of the *Domus Augustana*. It is a vast extended area (160 m x 48 m) with a shorter curved side. At either end are a couple of small semi-circular constructions, possibly fountains. The building was surrounded by a brick pillared portico of two storeys. The imperial box was half way along the eastern side. It was semi-circular and surrounded at the back by a vaulted two storied corridor, decorated with stucco lacunars. Three rooms still with their painted decoration open out from the lower part. On the shorter northern side some of the rooms were possibly used as dressing rooms or storage areas. It is not clear for what purpose the oval enclosure in the centre of the arena was used. It was erected at a later date, perhaps in the time of Theodoric, who was then living on the Palatine. During this period, a portico was also built in the centre of the Stadium, of which only the bases of the pillars remain.

55. The Stadium.
The imperial box

THE BUILDINGS UNDER THE DOMUS FLAVIA:
THE HOUSE OF THE GRIFFINS, THE AULA ISIACA
AND THE DOMUS TRANSITORIA

The structures discovered in different periods beneath the Flavians Palace are very important for reconstructing the ancient history of building on the Palatine.
The **House of the Griffins** ㉛, after long restoration work, is now finally open to the public. The paintings previously exhibited in the Museo Palatino have been restored to their place of origin. Furthermore, work carried out to ensure a greater stability of the building, have resulted in the recovery of another finely decorated room in the house, just to the north of the others. It is reached from the *Lararium* of the *Domus Flavia,* and is the oldest of the Republican houses on the Palatine. This building probably gives us the best idea of the typology and the decorations of the aristocratic residences of that time. It was built on two floors, each – it seems – with an independent entrance, using the original slope of the hill. The upper floor developed around an atrium, or peristyle, with an impluvium in peperino. Some fragments of mosaic still remain. They are black and white, with a pattern called *lithostroton* (a mixture of pebbles and coloured marbles).

At a later date, perhaps in the Augustean period, another structure was built on top of it. Part of a floor of marble slabs and some of the walls (with a different orientation to the later building) are still visible. The lower floor is reached by way of a steep staircase, part of which is ancient. There are eight rooms with walls in *opus*

incertum, restored in *opus reticulatum*. The painted decoration of the house is the oldest known in the Second Style, and confirms that it was built at the end of the 2nd century BC and restored around the middle of the 1st century BC. It was inhabited in Nero's time, as the brick walls testify, but vanished

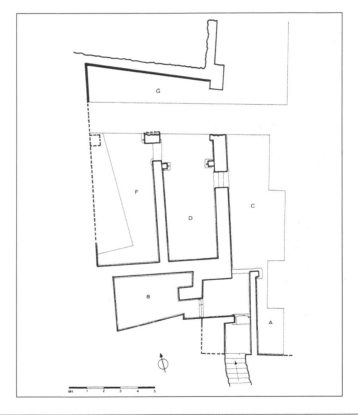

56. *The House of the Griffins. Lunette with the stuccoed griffins*

57. *Plan of the House of the Griffins*

under the new Palace buildings erected by the Flavians.

At the foot of the stairway, on the left, entrance is gained to a room with a double vaulted ceiling decorated in stucco (B). The room leans against the natural bedrock of the hill and has a black and white mosaic floor; light came from a skylight in the ceiling. The walls were painted with an architectural decoration of the Second Style: a low plinth of slim pillars is surmounted by columns, behind which are mirrors of fake polychrome marble, with rows of ashlar-work in perspective. An uninterrupted cornice runs along the top of the columns. Even the decoration in the next room (C), of which only the left wall remains (the others being the foundations of subsequent constructions) repeats the architectural decorative layout of the previous room, but in a simpler fashion: on top of a short plinth stands the podium and on top of that are set the large orthostates framed by various coloured bands. High up, the whole wall ends in a double cornice. The floor is of mosaics with intersecting square and rhombic patterns. The small room to the right (A), squeezed in between the wall in *opus reticulatum* and the Domitian foundations, is a later imitation of the same type of architectural decoration. Further along, on the left, is a cubicle (D) with well preserved walls. Here the decoration is more evolved than in the previous rooms, and is made up of three levels of differing depths: on the first is depicted a colonnade with a projecting plinth; on the second, a podium placed level with the plinths of the columns; and on the third a closed off wall, embellished with orthostates and mirrors of marquetry and inlaid marbles. High up is a cornice. An aedicula is painted in the alcove, flanked by two columns with a tympanum.

58. The House of the Griffins. Detail of the pictorial decoration in the Second Style

The same motif of cubes in perspective is to be found on the socle, as well as in the design in the centre of the floor. The following room (F) has suffered considerable damage. The left hand wall is in very bad condition due perhaps to some violent movement, such as an earthquake or ground subsidence. The floor, with a lozenge patterned mosaic, is dissected by a brick wall of Neronian times, possibly built after the fire of 64 AD and with a retaining function in mind. The pictorial decoration again has the same architectural design seen in the previous rooms, with fake marble encrustations divided into three parts. The vault was stuccoed with bands divided in squares and lozenges. The lunettes in the vault stand out due to the vividness of the red background and to the peculiarity of the decoration: two large griffins of white stucco stand in heraldic fashion before a flourishing acanthus

bush that fans out over the whole semi-circular space. Recent excavations, as already mentioned, have brought to light another room with an irregular plan (G), on the northern side, beyond the foundation wall of the *Lararium* above that dissects it. In the room, that together with the others closed the house off from the valley, is a lobby or entrance passage to the lower floor. The northern wall at the back also has bad subsidence problems. It was over seven metres long and had large windows at regular intervals, that gave light to the internal rooms as well. It was built in square tufa blocks (*opus quadratum*), mixed with *opus caementicium*, and a part in *opus reticulatum*. The painted decoration was the standard architectural type with a central perspective view, that of an illusory arcade, with columns and angular pillars rising up off a podium. At the back the still closed off wall has

little orthostates in various colours. There is a doric trabeation in the upper part, with triglyphs and *guttae* below. In the metope panels, bucranes alternate with lion heads and golden incensories. The portico is covered with a lacunar roof. The variety and refinement of the ornamentation distinguishes this particular room from the others, and place its pictorial decoration in a more advanced phase of the Second Style. From the Basilica, by way of a little stairway that has its left hand wall in *opus reticulatum* (A), it is possible to go down (though the access is closed to the public) to the so-called **Aula Isiaca** ㉜, a vast rectangular room (B) with its shorter side apsed in brick (C). This side was, in fact, added at a later date. This is all that remains of a large and sumptuous republican *domus*, with its interesting pictorial remains in the advanced Second Style. In Nero's time, a semi-circular cistern with four aisles was incorporated into the room. This can be reached by a modern stairway, for the whole the structure was buried beneath the Domitian Palace. The wall paintings in the *Aula Isiaca* were removed for conservation reasons, and have recently been restored. They are presently on show in one of the rooms of the *Domus Augustana*, known as the

59. The House of the Griffins. Detail of the pictorial decoration of the cubicle D

Loggia Mattei. To the right hand side, on entering this room, there is on display a fragment of the pictorial decorations found underneath the paintings of the apse while they were being removed. It is of the usual architectural design of the Second Style, and can therefore be dated to a preceding phase of the building, around the middle of the 1 century BC. The longer wall of the *Aula* is framed at its base by a socle and at the top by a rich cornice. The central part has an aedicula with panels on either side, inserted into architectural elements. These have a strong feeling of fantasy about them rather than a connotation of reality. The landscapes and scenes in the central *aedicula*, as well as the large central panel to the left are practically illegible. The right hand side is much better preserved. This was documented by drawings in the 18th century, partly stored in England, at Eton. The figures in the painting are participating in sacrificial rites near an altar, on which an eagle is pouring a liquid from a ritual vessel. At the top of the wall is a frieze decorated with lotus flowers, cobras and other objects sacred to the cult of Isis. On the shorter wall, in very bad condition, is a scene from the Trojan cycle: the arrival of Helen and Paris in Egypt. The lunette, with a

frieze similar to the previous one, has a golden *situla* decorated with roses, placed on top of a non-identified element. In the vault the artist has abandoned traditional themes and expresses himself with a freedom that is rarely seen in ancient decoration, as for example in the red ribbon that twines round a large blue band. Lotus flowers and rose leaves complete the decorative cornice, which was designed to frame the other scenes with symbols of Isis.

The apse is decorated with smaller panels depicting scenes from the Nile (pygmies, hippopotami) and larger panels representing a sacred landscape, framed by slender columns. There is also an altar with torches leaning against a rock and in the lower part ducks swimming in the waters of a fountain.

The paintings of the *Aula*, called *Isiaca* because of the many decorative motifs relating to the Isis' cult (a *situla*, a garland of roses in a little net, lotus flowers, a snake with a squashed body etc.), were initially dated to the time of Caligula, as this emperor was a devotee of the cult of the

ancient Egyptian goddess. Today, after a more accurate review, the date has been put back to the Augustean period. Under Augustus, motifs relating to Egypt and the cult of Isis were very fashionable following the victory at Actium. Deprived of any religious meaning, they were used as mere decorative elements.

The third and last complex buried under the *Domus Flavia* (visits only on request) is the one improperly called "**Livia's Bath**" ㉝. These constructions are actually from the time of Nero and relate in part to the *Domus Transitoria* and in part to the *Domus Aurea*. From the Triclinium of the *Domus Flavia*, down an ancient stairway (A) there is a space, now covered with skylights: on the left is a pavilion (C), which originally was decorated with polychrome columns and pillars and had a marble floor. There is a fountain in the centre and a niche at the back. The wall opposite is decorated with a graceful nymphaeum of two orders, partially reconstructed from drawings made during the excavations of the 1700s (B). The columns

60. Plan of the Aula Isiaca

61. The Aula Isiaca. Detail of the pictorial decoration with Egyptian and Isis motifs

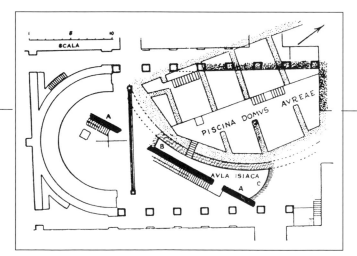

north-eastern side (F) have vaults decorated with various motifs. Often the paintings and golden stuccoes were made more precious by the use of glass paste in the decorations. The building seems to have had an upper floor, in fact the polychrome marble inlaid floor, that is to the west of the overhanging Nymphaeum and slightly lower than the Domitian level (now buried) was part of it.

The lavishness of the architecture and the decorations of these Neronian structures leaves no doubt in one's mind as to the truthfulness of Suetonius' description regarding the opulence of the *Domus Aurea*. In his desire to imitate the Hellenistic kings, Nero chose the language of grandeur, refinement and sumptuousness, to impress the crowds and also give a sacral justification to his absolute power. Above the structures of the *Domus Transitoria*, destroyed in the fire of 64 AD, were laid the foundations of the *Domus Aurea* (E). The building was never completed, but it was reused by Domitian to found his new palace. There

is also a large latrine (I) belonging to the Neronian phase, perhaps used by the workmen while the works were in progress. A long stone bench leans against the walls, with a series of seats next to one another, and a floor channel for the waste runs on the floor. From the peristyle it is possible to go down to the so-called *Mundus* (today not accessible to the public) which was unearthed by Giacomo Boni. This is a circular room built of tufa blocks and covered with a dome (*tholos*), that was most likely used as a granary.

were of *verde* and *rosso antico* marbles, and had bronze capitals. The water spurting from the fountains of the second order, was collected in a marble trough. Around it are several rooms (D), one of which, cut by the foundations of the *Domus Aurea,* still retains very beautiful paintings from the Trojan cycle (now on show in the Museo Palatino) and has its floor and walls veneered with coloured marbles. Two openings in the wall give onto two rooms containing original fountains with steps forming a series of small falls. The rooms on the

62. Domus Transitoria. Vault decorated with frescos and golden stucco-work

63. Domus Transitoria. Detail of the painted decoration and frieze (with scenes from the battle of the Amazons)

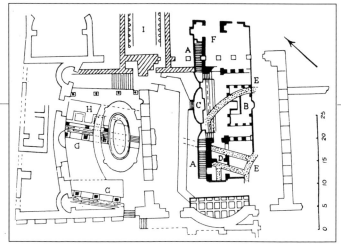

64. *Plan of the Domus Transitoria rooms commonly called "The Baths of Livia"*

65. *Panels inlaid with marble from walls of the Domus Transitoria. Rome, Museo Palatino*

66. *Aula Isiaca. Detail of the vault decoration*

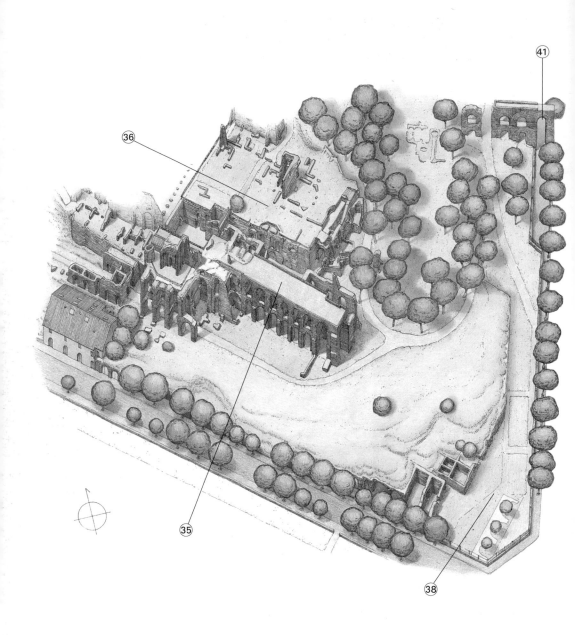

THE SLOPES ON THE SIDE OF THE VIA DEI CERCHI: THE SEVERAN COMPLEX, THE SEPTIZODIUM, THE PEDAGOGIUM AND THE SCHOLA PRAECONUM

This itinerary visits a series of monuments that in ancient times were extensions and logistical support spaces within the Palace, of which they formed an integral part.

The itinerary starts on the shorter northern side of the Stadium; there are some **brick buildings** ㉞ on the left hand side, leaning against the Convent of San Bonaventura, perhaps the remains of a nymphaeum or waterworks. By crossing the terrace that skirts the eastern side of the Stadium, the visitor reaches the Severan buildings, conventionally divided into Arcades (the outer part, in front of the Circus Maximus) and the Baths (the inner part, close to the Hippodrome).

From the highest part of the Baths, below and to the front, can be seen the **Arcades** ㉟. Even from a distance, they typify this side of the hill with their bare simple structures of impressive height. They have a double order of vaulted structures, supported on brick piers. They were built as supporting walls, but also to extend the hillside outwards, thereby creating an artificial platform on which to build the new wing of the Palace. Looking out from the terrace, where in ancient times stood

the most important part of the building, is one of the most impressive Roman panoramas: the view ranges from the Aventine to the Circus Maximus, and from Caracalla's Baths over to the Janiculum and Saint Peter's.

The **Baths** ㊱ are to be found on the eastern side of the Stadium, behind the exhedra,

67. Arcades and Severan Baths

68. Severan Arcades

and are called Severan from an item found in the *Historia Augusta*. They were several storeys high, and were excavated by the papal archaeologists under Pope Pius IX, and again in recent years. Investigations have shown that the plant for the thermal building goes back to Domitian, who must have decided that his Palace needed large Baths as well: the intermediate rooms, still partially buried, were built at the time of Domitian, although the real thermal buildings, in the upper part, were built at a later date and in various stages. The most important of these seem to date to the time of Septimius Severus, as proven by the brick stamps that have been found on site. Some parts, however, were built in the time of Maxentius, for the Cronographer of AD 354 writes: «*Thermas in Palatio fecit*». The presence, especially in the internal floors, of

partition walls, reinforced bracing and other restructuring of various kinds, are a further confirmation that the Severan buildings were not the product of a unitary project, but the result of several subsequent interventions. The building's thermal character is also confirmed by the presence of basins, drains and heating systems for both water and room temperature. The decoration of the rooms was very lavish, as can been inferred from the architectural remains: entire blocks of architraves, capitals and columns are still partially preserved in the rooms on the ground floor. Some important sculptures have also been found in the same area. Crossing the upper terrace of the Baths in the direction of the Circus Maximus, past a tall building (part of a stairway structure) and through an arcade that serves as a bridge, the visitor comes to the small **Baths of Maxentius** ㊲. These were built on a double row of

high vaulted structures, but what is left of this building lies partially buried, or covered by sheds in order to protect the lining of the basins and the clearly visible system of the *suspensurae*.
Behind the buildings of Maxentius, towards the Circus, is a small cylindrical construction. This might well be a latrine, though its function is not clear.
It was on this side that Septimius Severus built his new imperial box (*pulvinar*), which seems to be almost suspended in mid air. From his seat on the Palatine he could watch the performances down in the Circus Maximus. Down the pine covered road that runs along the eastern slope of the Palatine, the visitor arrives at the foot of the Arcades and of the Baths. From here it is not difficult to reach the south-eastern corner of the hill, where once stood a very famous monument, both in Antiquity and in the Middle Ages: the Severan **Septizodium** ㊳, a monumental facade of a nymphaeum, adorned with columns. It was completely demolished in 1588-1589 by order of Sistus V and the hand of Domenico Fontana, who reused the marble in various ways (for the Sistine Chapel of Santa Maria Maggiore for example). Today, after recent excavations have made it possible to precisely locate its

69. Pedagogium

70. Schola Praeconum. Mosaic with heralds

position, plans have been drawn up. It was about 90 metres long and had two lateral foreparts. In the centre columns flanked three large niches. Its marble decoration must have been very sumptuous: *giallo antico* and African marble alternated with granite, while exhedras with fountains and sculptures stood in between the columns. Recent excavations have brought to light a colossal lying headless statue that came from the central exhedra and probably personified the Tiber. This building, depicted in many Renaissance drawings, was built on the Palatine slopes, according to the anonymous author of the *Historia Augusta*, so that travellers coming from the Appian Way could take in at a glance the splendour of the city (the *Urbs*), and especially that of the Imperial Palace. Walking along at the foot of the Arcades with the Circus Maximus on the left, past the wide

hemicycle of the *Domus Augustana*, the visitor comes to the **Pedagogium** ㊴, which was a school for imperial slaves. This was built in Domitian' times, and had a double row of small rooms (one with an apse) that were plastered and paved with mosaics. They were arranged around a peristyle, reassembled by Canina in an arbitrary way, reusing some elegant trabeations that did not even belong to the building. The name derives from some graffiti, that date from a time not earlier than the Severan period, found in one of the rooms, in which the phrase "*exit de paedagogio*" followed by the slave's name is repeated over and over again. The most famous of these graffiti is the one that represents a crucifix with a donkey's head and the Greek inscription: "Alexamenos adores his god".
Another building of the Severan period is to be found between the *Pedagogium* and the Circus Maximus. This is a

porticoed courtyard with three vaulted rooms on the northern side. One of them has walls covered with a series of full scale male figures, only recently replaced in their original setting. As the floor mosaic also represents a procession of eight men bearing a standard, this room is referred to as the **Schola Praeconum** ㊵, that is to say the seat of the corporation of heralds.
From this point, it is possibile to choose between two paths. The visitor can either continue along the road to the south-western corner of the Palatine, with the little centrally planned Church of San Teodoro at his back and return to the *Domus Tiberiana* along the Victory *Clivus;* or, and this is preferable for a more thorough visit, he can go back to the Severan Arcades and from there cover the eastern slope of the Palatine in the direction of the Coliseum, keeping the Caelian still to the right.

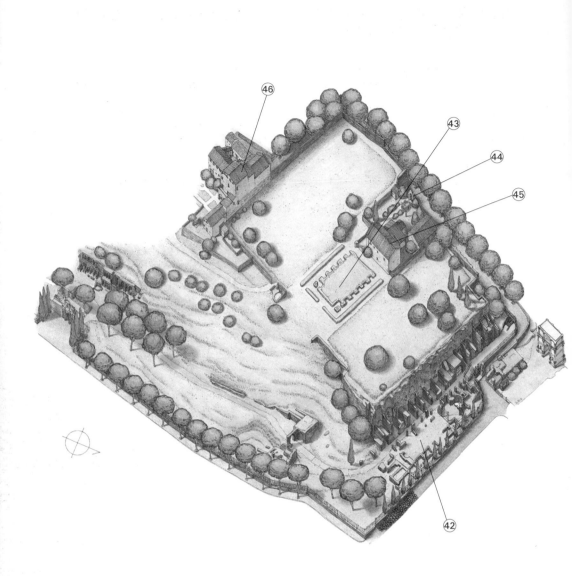

42 "Baths of Elagabalus"
43 Temple (of the Sun?)
44 *Pentapylum*
45 Church of San Sebastiano
46 Church of San Bonaventura

THE SLOPES IN THE DIRECTION OF VIA DI SAN GREGORIO. THE BARBERINI VINEYARD

Continuing along the grassy slopes, under the pine trees, the visitor passes not far from the last arch of the **Aqueduct of Claudius** ㊶, which was extended as far as the Palatine by Domitian in order to provide his Palace with a plentiful water supply. On the left are some brick buildings, perhaps water distribution plants. The itinerary goes on keeping to the right of the Palatine entrance on via di San Gregorio, where Vignola's portal – the original position of which was in the Farnese Gardens – has been erected. On the left are the remains of some vaulted buildings, probably substructions, as yet unexplored.

On the side of the hill, on the left, there are some remnants of floors in *opus*

*71. Arcades of the
Aqueduct of Claudius*

spicatum and some hydraulic covers in potsherd; further down on the right is a group of structures (one with an apsed room) which are presently under excavation.

At the point where it is possible to see the base of the Temple of Venus and Rome, the road bends. On the left soars a multi-storied building that supports the Barberini Vineyard, and dates to the Flavian era, with later restorations of the 3rd century AD. To the right are the remains of a complex, the name and function of which is uncertain, even though some have identified it as the **Baths of Elagabalus** ㊷. It is the central apsed room with its fountains that draws the most attention: the hall, perhaps originally part of the Baths, was probably converted into a shrine in Late Antiquity. Further along, past the remains of a flint surface on which rose the *Turris Chartularia*, the visitor turns left and a few stairs later is on the grassy terrace of the Barberini Vineyard (110 m x 150 m). Excavations by Alfonso Bartoli in the '30s brought to light the foundations of a **Temple** ㊸ (60 m x 40 m). Its identification is controversial, but most scholars believe it to be the Temple of the Sun, built by Elagabalus close to the Imperial Palaces. The Temple, of which only the foundations remain, was surrounded by a portico. In this temple Elagabalus set up the Trojan Palladium, along with other sacred objects. It was perhaps because of this that the area was called "Pallara" in the Middle Ages. The building remained standing until the Late Antiquity, as testified by several ancient authors. It was entered through five monumental barrel-vaults called *Pentapylum* ㊹. The remains of this construction can be seen on via San Bonaventura, at the entrance to the **Church of San Sebastiano** ㊺, part of which stands on the pavement that once surrounded the temple. The "Acts of Saint Sebastian's martyrdom" recount that the saint, when brought to

The Temple of the Sun

«On entering the city, Elagabalus immediately dedicated a temple to himself in the guise of the Sun, *iuxta aedes imperatorias*, and there he placed all the objects sacred to the Romans, such as the *acus Magnae Matris*, Vesta's sacred fire, the Palladium, and the shields of Mars. This, so that no other god but himself could be worshipped in Rome» (The authors of the *Historia Augusta*, *Life of Elagabalus*, 3, 4).

72. Portal from the Farnese Gardens reassembled in via di San Gregorio

trial before the Emperor Diocletian, addressed him standing *"super gradus Heliocabulli"*. The temple must have been connected by the *"gradus"* to the *Clivus Palatinus*.

On the southern side of the Barberini Vineyard, on top of an enormous *castellum aquae*, that must once have supplied the Severan Baths with water, stands the **Church of San Bonaventura** ㊻, that was built, together with the annexed convent, by Cardinal Francesco

73. *Aerial view of the Barberini Vineyard*

74. *The Barberini Vineyard. Church of San Sebastiano*

THE MUSEO PALATINO

The first Antiquarium on the Palatine goes back to the second half of the 19th century and was set up by Pietro Rosa in the *Domus Tiberiana*, on the ground floor of a building belonging to the Farnese, along the Victory *Clivus*. The building – and therefore the Museum – was demolished by Rodolfo Lanciani in 1882, during work carried out to reunify the archaeological areas of the Forum and the Palatine by removing the Farnese boundary wall. With no Museum, all the most important material recovered from excavations on the hill from that moment onwards were taken to the Museo delle Terme di Diocleziano. In the '30s a new Palatine Antiquarium was established by Alfonso Bartoli in the Convent built by the Sisters of the Visitation in 1868 on the summit of the hill. The new Museum, housed in the same building as that of today, only made use of the first floor for exhibiting its most important finds, its new acquisitions and those from the Museo delle Terme. After the war, and Bartoli's death, in an attempt to increase the importance of the Museo Nazionale

Romano in comparison with that of the Palatine, it was decided – not without harsh words – that all the finds of major artistic importance should go to the former, whereas elements of topographical importance, those more precisely connected to the site and its monuments, should stay in the Museo Palatino. At the end of the '60s the Antiquarium was again restored and consolidated, including a new museum

layout which had but a short life. After a long period of closure when all the sculptures previously exhibited at the Museo delle Terme had been recuperated, the Antiquarium was finally reopened to the public. It now has a new itinerary which shows – besides the necessary *excursus* on Rome at the time of Romulus – the artistic culture of the Imperial Palaces from the time of Augustus up until the Late Empire.

75. View of the Museo Palatino

76. Square altar with deities (Venus, Mercury, Minerva and perhaps Felicitas), probably of the Flavian period, found during the excavations of the 1800s on the site of the Stadium.

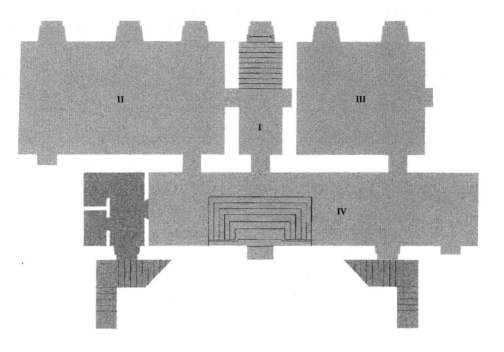

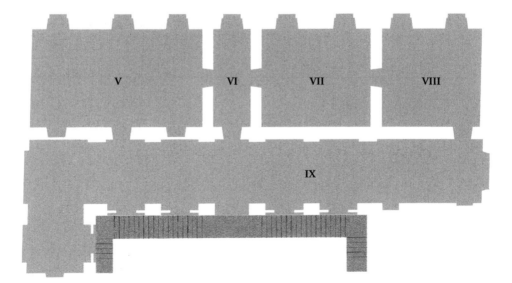

THE GROUND FLOOR

**The Palatine from its origins
to the Republican age**

ROOM I
Prehistory of the hill (from 100,000 years ago
to the end of the second millennium BC).
From the Palaeolithic to the Bronze Age.

ROOMS II-III
Protohistory of the hill (10th-7th century
BC). Huts and burials of the Iron Age.

ROOM IV
Archaic and Republican ages (6th-1st century
BC). Cultural units and private *domus*.

THE FIRST FLOOR

The Palatine in imperial times

ROOM V
The Augustan period (29 BC-14 AD).
Sanctuary of Apollo Aziacus and decorative
themes for the glorification of the Principality.

ROOM VI
The Neronian period (54-68 AD). *Domus
Transitoria* and the new decorative concepts.

ROOMS VII-VIII
From the Julio-Claudian emperors (1st
century AD) to the Tetrarchy (3rd-4th century
AD). Official portraiture and Palace
decoration.

ROOM IX
Sculptural decoration of the Palace. Greek
originals and Roman copies of Classical and
Hellenistic works.

Rooms I-II-III. The Prehistory and Protohistory of the hill

The brick masonry and the concrete foundations which can be seen all over the whole of the ground floor belong to the "reception" area of the grandiose Palace, the *Domus Flavia*. More specifically, the back structures in rooms III-IV belong to one of the two elliptical Nymphaei flanking the sumptuous Triclinium, standing at the exit of the Museum on the left hand side.

The considerable remains from the various buildings of the Augustan and Julio-Claudian period are on display in room III.

A small part of the remains from a large construction, built after 64 AD, in the time of Nero, is visible in room IV. The rooms house the earliest archaeological documentation so far recovered on the Palatine, from the Prehistory to the Archaic period. Many hand made stone objects found on the Palatine suggest that the area was sparsely inhabited from the Middle Palaeolithic Age (100,000-35,000 years ago), through to the Upper Palaeolithic Age (35,000-10,000 years ago).

The existence of a permanent settlement on the hill can be dated back to the Late Bronze Age (13th century BC and the first half of the 12th century BC), whereas the main occupancy of the Palatine is documented to the beginning of the Iron Age (900-830 BC: phase IIA of the Latium culture).

▲ *Funeral artefacts found in a child's tomb on the northern slopes of the Palatine, together with the remains of four huts and an oven sunk in the clay. These structures, from the middle of the 9th century BC and the end of the 8th century BC, were abandoned at the time of the construction of a wall of earth and tufa chips, identified by archaeologists as the ring of fortifications around the city of Romulus.*

▼ *Artefacts from an incineration tomb of the 9th century BC, recovered in 1954 during excavations at the House of Livia. The tomb took the form of a cylindrical well, inside which was a large "dolium" with a round lid. Inside there was a spherical urn with a lid in the shape of a hut, and the remains of the funeral vessels (ceramics and bronze miniatures).*
The tomb dates to phase IIA of the Latium culture (900-830 BC) and its typology is similar to the burials of the necropolis in the Forum.

Room IV. The Archaic and Republican ages (6th-1st centuries BC)

In the Archaic period several sacred buildings must have existed on the summit of the hill, as architectural terracottas and antefixes in the Etruscan style recovered from excavations seem to suggest. Two terracotta heads, perhaps belonging to the fronton decoration, found in the *favissae* (the sacred ditches) of the Temple of Victory, are now on display in the show-cases. The historical and religious importance of the Palatine was such that in republican times the area became a desirable place for the residences of the Roman upper class. Only some peperino and stucco capitals from the *domus* are on display in the Museum. They are interesting both for the materials and techniques.

◀ *Altar to an "unknown god", found in 1829 on the southwestern side of the Palatine near the Velabrum. Engraved on it is the following inscription: "Consecrated to both a god and a goddess and erected by Gaius Sextus, son of Gaius Calvinus, praetor, by decree of the Senate". Some scholars connect the altar to the sanctuary of Aius Locutius, the mysterious deity who had given the Romans advance warning of the Gallic invasion of 390 BC.*

▲ *Antefixes with the head of Juno Sospita, found on the site of the Temple of the "Magna Mater", from the first decades of the 5th century BC. A blue helmet with the horns and ears of a goat adorns the head of the goddess. Antefixes similar to these have also been found elsewhere, in Rome and in Latium.*

Room V. The Augustan period (29 BC - 14 AD)

The character and aspect of the Palatine underwent a total change with the arrival of Octavian. Following a strong intuition, and in order to develop his political programme in a difficult period of transition, Octavian – founder of a new Rome – used a figurative language based on the choice of precise symbols and above all of those deities who seemed to better represent his policy.

Augustus' deepest and most long lasting identification was with Apollo, defender of morality and order, of moderation and peace. The god's almost obsessive image is repeated over and over again in the architectural terracotta on display, in which another Apollonian symbol appears, that of the *betilus*. This is a non iconic image of the deity, in the form of a cone adorned with Phoebus' lyre and Diana's quiver.

▲ ◄ *Polychrome terracotta tablets found in 1968 during excavations on the site of the Temple of Apollo. The first one depicts the quarrel between Apollo and Heracles concerning the ownership of the delphic tripod. Apollo holds a bow and two arrows in his left hand, while Heracles is brandishing a club. At the base of the tripod, between their feet, is represented the "omphalos" at Delphi.*
On the second one two priestesses facing one another are decorating a central object with ribbons: this is a "betilus" (non iconic image of Apollo), set on a high pedestal and embellished below with the symbols of the god: the lyre, the bow and the quiver.

▲ *Three female hermae in "nero antico" marble found by Rosa in 1869 in the area around the Temple of Apollo. It has recently been suggested that these three statues were part of the fifty Danaids who, according to ancient sources, decorated the portico of the Augustan sanctuary.*

◄ *Small statue of an ephebe found by P. Rosa in the cryptoporticus to the east of the Temple of Apollo. The victorious young athlete bearing a crown is sculpted in basalt in imitation of a precious bronze. It was probably part of a decorative programme commissioned by Octavian after his victory at Actium in 31 BC.*

Room VI. The Neronian period (54-68 AD)

Under Nero architectural dimensions, building criteria, and general town planning arrangements, underwent remarkable changes. The structures of the *Domus Transitoria*, still visible below the *Domus Flavia* that obliterated them completely, show in every detail the pompous ostentation that, in the wake of the Ptolemians, Nero displayed as a guaranty for a prosperous and contented government. The use of gold and gems, criticised by Lucan, can be clearly seen in the painted rooms of the Palatine.

Wall paintings from a very rich nymphaeum under the triclinium of the "Domus Flavia" which, in ancient times, was part of the "Domus Transitoria". The decoration of the room was extremely sumptuous, with the floor and walls inlaid with precious coloured marbles, and the vaults decorated with glass paste marquetry, to such an extent that Suetonius recounts: "Everything was covered with gold, precious stones and mother of pearl" (Nero, 31).

On the vaults are depicted scenes from episodes of the Trojan cycle: the wounding of Telephus and the quarrel over Achilles' weapons. Epic themes also appear in the decoration of the lunettes: the theft of Rhesus' horses, and Ulysses and Neoptolemus in Scyros. Generally the artist Fabullus is regarded as the author of the paintings. He is remembered by Pliny for his extreme composure (wearing his toga even on the scaffolding) and for his style defined as "floridus" and "humidus".

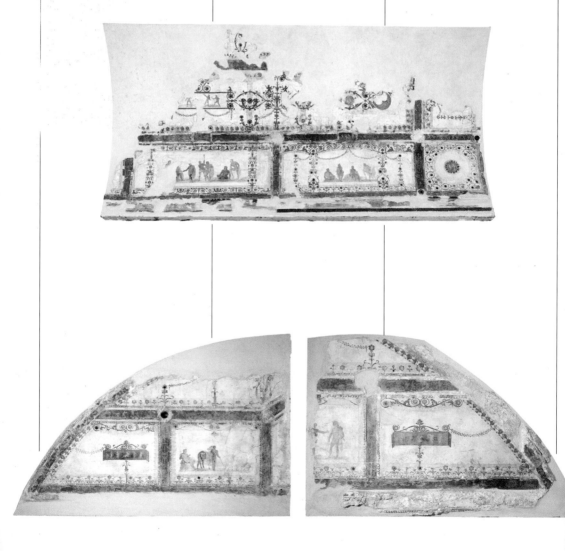

Rooms VII - VIII. From the Julio-Claudian emperors to the Tetrarchy (1st-4th centuries AD)

Changes in taste and culture regarding the Imperial *Domus* up until the decline of the late centuries are displayed in these two rooms. The material on show at least gives an idea of the Palaces' refined luxury, where magnificence played an important part in imperial ceremonies.

Both the structures and the finishes were often made of coloured marble slabs, especially *giallo antico* and *pavonazzetto* marbles. Even the walls, as previously mentioned regarding the *Domus Transitoria*, were sometimes inlaid with marble *crustae* that created refined complex patterns.

Numerous portraits, mostly of emperors or members of the imperial family, use a classical and idealised language to reinforce the idea that not only was the *Palatium* the centre of power, but also that the imperial cult was the principal element of this power.

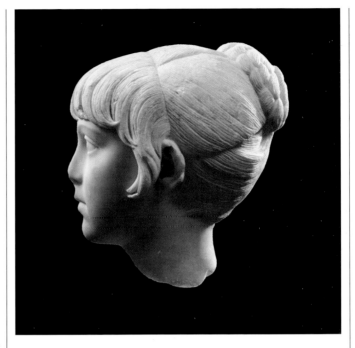

▲ *Portrait of a young princess, from the Palatine Stadium. For a long time thought to be the portrait of Faustina the Younger, wife of the Emperor Marcus Aurelius, but now considered to be one of his daughters. It is of great workmanship, and perhaps from the hand of an Attic artist.*

▶ *Portrait of Nero discovered by Pietro Rosa in the eastern wing of the cryptoporticus supporting the sacred area of the Temple of Apollo. Regarded as one of the most precious portraits of Nero, it is characterised by the solid head of the Domitii and a short partly incised beard, by the rather flabby fleshiness of the face and the haircut with locks hanging down over the forehead, as was the fashion of the time.*

Room IX. The sculptural decoration of the Palace

The sculptures exhibited in the Museum were essentially made to embellish the imperial *Domus,* but they also had the political aim to impress anybody entering the Palace. The extremely high quality of the finds on show clearly reflects the prestigious patron who commissioned them, that is to say the imperial family.

The emperors, in the same way as rich collectors, loved to possess copies of Greek masterpieces, especially from the 4th century BC. Sculptures by Praxiteles, the most praised and reproduced of all the artists, were particularly appreciated by the Romans. So too were the sculptors Skopas, Lysippus and Polyclitus, artists of the Severan and Hellenistic periods.

On the whole, the statues in the Museum – deities, athletes, muses and other ideal figures – sum up the symbolic value that the *Palatium* represented as the centre of the representation of imperial charisma and power organisation.

◀ *Small statue of a satyr staring at his own tail. This is a small genre sculpture, designed for a courtyard or a garden, and derived from an original bronze of the Hellenistic period. The head is a plaster cast of the replica which is in Florence.*

▶ *Statue of Aura from the Palatine slopes. The beautiful sculpture, similar to the figure in the Temple of Apollo in Phigalia, is considered to be one of the original acroteria of that complex. It is the work of Paionios of Mende and perhaps was reused for the same function in one of the sacred buildings on the Palatine.*

▶ Statue of the so-called "Dancer", found in 1935 during Bartoli's excavations at the Domus Augustana. The posture of the girl, with her (missing) head turned to the right and her shoulders thrown backwards, was considered by many scholars to be that of a dancer similar to the Spartan dancers with a "kalathiskos", who wore a typical short chiton. It is copied from an original bronze of the classical era, and is from the time of Hadrian.

▲ Torso of Artemis found underneath one of the Severan Arcades, close to the Circus Maximus. It derives from a Pergamon original of the Late Hellenistic period, and is from the time of Antoninus.

C. L. Visconti, R. Lanciani,
Guida del Palatino, Roma 1873.

R. Lanciani, *Il "Palazzo Maggiore"
nei secc. XVI-XVIII,* "Bullettino
dell'Instituto", 9, 1894, p. 3 f.

E. Haugwitz, *Palatin, seine
Geschichte und seine Ruinen,*
Roma 1901.

H. Jordan, Ch. Hülsen,
*Topographie der Stadt Rom im
Altertum,* I, 3, Berlin 1907,
p. 29 f.

S.B. Platner, Th. Ashby, *A
Topographical Dictionary of Ancient
Rome,* Oxford-London 1929.

G. Lugli, *Roma antica, il centro
monumentale,* Roma 1946,
p. 389 f.

G. Carettoni, *Itinerario del
Palatino,* Bologna 1947.

P. Romanelli, *Il Palatino,*
Roma 1950.

G. Lugli, *Regio Urbis Decima.
Mons Palatinus. Fontes,*
Roma 1960.

G. Carettoni, *Il Palatino nel
Medioevo,* "Studi Romani", 9,
1961, p. 508 f.

B. Tamm, *Auditorium and
Palatium,* Stockholm 1963.

G. Wataghin Cantino, *La Domus
Augustana,* Torino 1966.

P. Castren, H. Lilius, *Graffiti
del Palatino* (Acta Inst. Romani
Finlandiae), Helsinki 1970.

F. Coarelli, *Guida archeologica
di Roma,* Roma 1975.

F. Coarelli, Roma (Guide
archeologiche Laterza),
Roma-Bari 1995².

Gli Orti Farnesiani sul Palatino,
Roma 1990.

M. A. Tomei, *Il Palatino,*
Roma 1992.

L. Richardson jr., *A New
Topographical Dictionary of Ancient
Rome,* Baltimore-London 1992.

E. M. Steinby (a cura di),
*Lexicon Topographicum Urbis
Romae,* I-III, Roma 1993-1996.

Electa Guides for the
Soprintendenza Archeologica
di Roma

Series edited by
Rosanna Cappelli

THE PALATINE

Text
Maria Antonietta Tomei

Translation
Luisa Guarneri Hynd

Printed in 1998 on behalf
of Elemond Spa by
Tipografica La Piramide (Roma)